HANNS LILJE

THE
VALLEY
OF THE
SHADOW

TRANSLATED
AND WITH AN INTRODUCTION BY
OLIVE WYON

FORTRESS PRESS
Philadelphia

First published 1950 by Fortress Press

Second-third printings 1950
Fourth-fifth printings 1951
Sixth-eighth printings 1952
Ninth-thirteenth printings 1953
Fourteenth printing 1954

First Fortress Press paperback edition 1966

Second printing 1967
Third printing 1977

Library of Congress Catalog Card Number 76-55522

ISBN 0-8006-1699-5

6202L76   Printed in U.S.A.   1-1699

PREFACE TO THE NEW EDITION

It is a joy for me to know that this little book is being made available once again. The new edition is proof of the continuing interest in its message. I hope that for many readers it will help to fortify their faith in Christ. Young people may be particularly interested in a personal story emanating from the time of the Third Reich. May that story help them learn how to stand fast in times of trial. 'For God, who answered me in the day of my distress, was with me in the way which I went.' (Genesis 35.3.)

Hanover, Germany
Christmas, 1976

HANNS LILJE

CONTENTS

In the distance, dark and dim,
Hangs a heavy veil. Bow your heart
In silent reverence.
Above, the silence of the stars,
Below, the silence of the grave.

GOETHE

With him is strength and wisdom: the
deceived and the deceiver are his. . . .
He discovereth deep things out of
darkness, and bringeth out to light the
shadow of death.

THE BOOK OF JOB. 12.16, 22

INTRODUCTION

HANNS LILJE is a well-known figure in the Ecumenical Movement. It was in August 1948, at Amsterdam, that I met him again, after an interval of several years. At this First Assembly of the World Council of Churches Bishop Lilje was the Chairman of Section I: *The Universal Church in God's Design.* He presided over this gathering of Bishops, theologians and Church leaders from all parts of the world with such dignity, humour and competence that it seemed almost impossible to realize that this able and attractive chairman had endured the horrors and perils of imprisonment under the Nazi régime, only four years before. Yet when we talked together in private, I had a glimpse of what those months of trial—literally under 'the Shadow of Death'—had meant to him.

His story is very moving; and its force is heightened by its restraint. It is possible, however, that we may miss some of the point of the narrative owing to our lack of knowledge of events inside Germany during the last year of the Nazi régime. A great deal more, however, is now known about that whole 'fantastic and tragical episode', and much that was perplexing has become clear. We owe this greater clarity to a number of writers, both German and English, who have given us first-hand accounts of different parts of the story of those years. Of course these accounts do not always agree with each other; for the period was so confused and so confusing, and contact between enemies of the régime was almost impossible. But out of these narratives we can build some kind of picture of the situation in Germany during those later years of the War.

The story begins on a glorious August day in 1944. Why

was Lilje arrested? As the prison gates closed behind him, we feel as bewildered as he felt on that strange day. The clue to the whole chain of events in this personal narrative lies in the political situation inside Germany during the War, and especially during the last months, when the final catastrophe was foreshadowed, and the inevitable day of reckoning was drawing near.

We are now aware that the German Resistance Movement was far more extensive, both before and during the War, than we were able to know at the time. The Nazi leaders were determined that no hint of such opposition should reach the outside world, and on the whole, they were successful. Further, it was in the interests of the opponents of the régime to keep their activities quiet; for they knew that if one name reached the ears of the Gestapo, not only that man, but numbers of his comrades would suffer torture and death. Nevertheless, the resistance was widespread.

In Great Britain we heard chiefly about the resistance offered by the Churches. In 1933, after the first shock of bewilderment was over, Catholics and Protestants alike stood out boldly 'in defence of the Gospel' and the dignity of man. Indeed, the Churches were the first group to show the National Socialist government that there were limits to the brutal exercise of power. The authorities might control the greater part of human life in Germany, but they now learned—to their great exasperation—that they could *not* control 'man's unconquerable mind'. They found they could not crush faith in God or love to man. Priests and pastors were in the forefront of the conflict. They suffered severely and heroically. We do not know how many died in concentration camps, but it is said that at least two thousand R.C. priests died for their faith in Dachau alone. Protestant resistance was equally fine in quality, both among the clergy and the laity. The name of Niemöller is known everywhere, but there are many others who suffered much, and risked everything for the sake of fidelity to Christ and His Church. Dietrich Bonhoeffer, a young theologian, is one example, He was arrested in 1943. He endured nobly and never betrayed a single comrade. He was killed just before the end came in 1945. Many more, whose names we shall never know, endured to the end with the same heroic faith. The present story is a classic instance of this 'spiritual resistance' fought with spiritual weapons alone.

Resistance began very early in sporadic groups, often working on parallel lines. In different forms, it spread all over the country, among the workers, and in the universities, among Social Democrats and Communists. University professors (several names are known to us in this circle; for instance, Karl Jaspers, E. R. Curtius, Romano Guardini, Constantin v. Dietze, Eduard Spranger, Gerhard Ritter), high officials in the government (especially in the Foreign Office), and men and women of high social standing were also deeply involved. Many were discovered and executed during the early stages of the War. For all who took an active part in this resistance it was a Reign of Terror.

In spite of this, however, groups sprang up and lived an intense life; their members wanted to prove that there was 'another Germany'.

A number of individuals are mentioned in this narrative, all of whom, in their differing ways, were opposed to the National Socialist régime and 'all its works'. There were, for instance, two brothers of a noble family, Werner and Fritz von der Schulenburg; Fritz was a high official in the government; Werner had been at one time German Ambassador to Russia. Had the July Plot succeeded, it would have been his task to make contact with Stalin immediately. Ewald von Kleist is mentioned by Lilje with warm appreciation. From other sources we learn how deeply this man impressed those who met him in prison. At his so-called 'Trial' he said openly: 'I have always fought against Hitler and the National Socialist régime with all the means in my power! I have never made any secret of it! I believe God wished me to act thus. God alone will be my Judge! ' Both at his trial and at his execution a few weeks later, friends and enemies alike were moved with admiration and respect by his spirit and his behaviour.

Among the young intellectuals Albrecht Haushofer was well known as a poet. His *Moabiter Sonette*—a poem on life in the Moabit Prison in Berlin—is famous. His father, a professor, knew Hess and Hitler well; the young poet therefore had no illusions about the Hitler régime. He tried to foster opposition *within* Nazi circles. His motives and actions were often misunderstood, but both Hitler and Himmler were well aware of his real sentiments; they pursued him with their vengeance; he was tracked down by the Gestapo and shot at the Lehrter Railway Station in Berlin on the 23rd of April, 1945, with his poem, the *Moabiter Sonette,* in his hands.

The name of Constantin von Dietze often occurs in this narrative. He is another instance of the type of man feared and hated by the Nazis. Born in 1891, he studied law and economics in various universities, including Cambridge. Later, he became a University Professor; he is now at Freiburg, where he has recently been Rector (Vice-Chancellor). He has also received the honorary degree of D.D. from Heidelberg, although he is an economist. He was involved in the preparations for Amsterdam, and was finally able to be there as a delegate. He was thrown into prison partly as a friend of Goerdeler's, and partly because he had worked out a new plan for the economic life of Germany—for future use. He had no connection with the 20th July Plot. He endured much during his months in prison; he was tortured, but refused to betray his friends.

Then there was Friedrich Justus Perels, legal adviser to the Confessional Church. He was a convinced Christian, and an enemy of all compromise, a 'magnificent character' The Gestapo loathed him. He was executed on the 23rd April, 1945, at the age of 34. His faith and courage were unshaken to the end.

One of the most important groups in the Resistance was that known as the *Kreisauer Kreis*. Its leaders were *Helmuth, Graf v. Moltke* and *Peter, Graf York v. Wartenberg*. The members of this group indeed constituted an *élite*: they were men of the highest character and ideals, with no axe of their own to grind. Their one thought was the highest welfare of their people in the sight of God. These men and women were not only concerned to oppose Hitler and all his works. They had a positive creative aim; they were determined to lay a foundation on which a new and better Germany could rise on the ruins of the old. Both Moltke and York were representatives of that nobility which combined love of country and a sense of responsibility for the nation with a wide European outlook and a deep religious faith.

Many of the members of this group are mentioned by Lilje in his narrative: *Gerstenmaier*, a Lutheran minister, and an active worker in the Ecumenical movement; *Poelchau*, who was Prison Chaplain at the Tegel Prison in Berlin; during the long years of the Nazi régime he stood by countless political prisoners, and later by his personal friends, to the hour of death. Constantly, at great personal risk, he managed to keep prisoners and their relatives in contact with one another. Many political prisoners of all nations, and many persecuted Jews, received comfort and help from this devoted man. *Theodor Steltzer* was a leading Protestant layman; he was greatly interested in the international aspect of the Lutheran Church; in 1933 he joined the General Staff of the Army. During the War he was sent to Norway; there, through his friendship with Bishop Berggrav and other leaders of the Church in the Scandinavian countries, he carried on—secretly and illegally of course—the struggle against National Socialism. *Adam von Trott zu Solz* was a highly gifted man who had lived and studied abroad for several years; he had been at Oxford, and later went to China. His years abroad had taught him to look at Germany objectively; when he had to return home he threw himself heart and soul into the Resistance Movement. *Theodor Haubach*, a leading Social Democrat, also belonged to this group.

Moltke himself made a deep impression on all who knew him. One who was with him at the concentration camp of Ravensbruck says that he can never forget him. He brought much strength and help to his fellow-prisoners by his human sympathy and understanding, his readiness to help, and by his detachment from personal and earthly interests which was due to the fact that he was already at home in a higher realm. His calmness and composure were so marked that his enemies were infuriated, and he was subjected to all kinds of indignities; he bore all with the same noble patience.

Moltke was condemned to death on the 10th of January, 1945. The letter in which he tells his wife of the sentence is a most moving and revealing document.[1] He tells his wife how glad he is that it has come out plainly at the trial that he and his closest friends had rejected the use of violence to further their aims; all they had done was to 'think'. He refers especially to Delp, Gerstenmaier and himself, and says: 'And it is the *thought* of these three solitary men which has given the Nazi leaders such a shock that they are determined to stamp out every trace of such thought! Isn't this a compliment if ever there was one?' He analyses the reasons for his condemnation to death and points out to his wife—and asks her to pass it on—that these are simply and solely 'spiritual', i.e. that he, Father

[1] An English translation of this letter appeared in *The Round Table*, June 1946, pp. 224-230.

Delp (S.J.), and Gerstenmaier had no personal interests to defend, nor would they consent to the use of violence; they were to be executed solely because they dared to *think*, and to *think in human and Christian terms*.[1]

Among the active political opponents of the Nazi régime no name is more important than that of *Carl Friedrich Goerdeler*. He was born in 1884, and took up the Law as his profession. After the first World War he occupied a high position as chief Bürgermeister of Leipzig. His work was very difficult under the Hitler régime, and in 1937 he resigned his office, and began to work with great intelligence and enthusiasm to free his country from its bondage. He was indeed *the* man of the Resistance Movement, occupying a key position. Before the War he travelled a great deal, and he made no secret of the fact that he thought it would be 'lunatic' for Germany to go to war. But he was a 'voice crying in the wilderness' and his warnings went unheeded.

This turn of events drove him to a deeper and more determined resistance to the régime itself. He worked hard for its overthrow. As a convinced Christian, for a long time he was against the use of violence. It was only when the situation became acute that he reluctantly came to the conclusion that Hitler must be assassinated. But he was no political fanatic. Rather he was a cultured lawyer and man of the world who thought and planned for a 'new Germany' on sound lines and with respect for freedom and the dignity of human beings; in the plans of those who were looking to the future Goerdeler was marked out as the future Chancellor of the Reich.

From the political point of view, however, the most

[1] Moltke was executed. Owing to delay on the part of the authorities and the confusion at the end of the War, Delp and Gerstenmaier were saved. Gerstenmaier is now at the head of the relief work of the Lutheran Church in Germany and was at Amsterdam.

effective and determined opposition came from the Army itself. Even during the early days of the War many Army leaders were against Hitler. Now and again, even in Russia, they tried to modify some of the worst of his orders. In March 1943 the Army Resistance group had already decided to kill Hitler.[1] The attempt was made and failed, owing to some mechanical error; the bomb did not explode, and the plot was never detected.

The Army leaders were determined to try again. Hitler was aware that the officers on his General Staff were 'difficult' and he was often suspicious of them, but he had no idea of what was actually going on in their minds. As the former officer who led the conspiracy against Hitler had been removed from his office, the Army group sought for someone else to carry out their purpose. They found him in the person of *Count Schenk von Stauffenberg*. The Stauffenbergs are an old South German Catholic family. This young officer was a member of the General Staff and was well known as a good organizer and administrator. Owing to serious injuries received in the campaign in North Africa, Stauffenberg was retained on the General Staff, in spite of his comparative youth. But Stauffenberg was more than a military expert. He read poetry and reflected on ultimate questions; he was a Christian, and he was opposed to Hitler for religious and for moral reasons. To his fellow-officers he seemed to be cut out as their 'leader' in this fresh stage of the Resistance Movement.

To speak of *the* Resistance Movement is perhaps a misnomer. The situation was rather that there were a great many groups, of varying kinds and sizes and influence, which were all opposed to the régime, but for various reasons. Many of them were 'eliminated' by the Gestapo

---

[1] This was not their final effort. As early as 1938 the Army leaders had decided to get rid of Hitler. 'Munich', however, made them pause.

and many men and women—persons of the highest character and intelligence—were put to death long before the end of the War was in sight. They gave their lives for the cause of freedom and justice. As the political situation became acute it was evident that the Military Group, composed mainly of officers of high rank, held the key to the situation. They alone had access to Hitler in a special way; they alone would not shrink from the use of force. Hitler was continually in conflict with the Army General Staff, for it was 'the one dissident group which he could neither dissolve nor eliminate', and, adds Trevor-Roper, it was the one group which at one time 'might have eliminated him'.

Thus this widespread—but largely unorganized—opposition culminated in the *Generals' Plot of July 20th, 1944*, an event in which, however, many opponents of the régime took no part, and of which they had no certain knowledge. A small, determined, and influential group alone undertook to conspire against Hitler's life.

Thus it was just two months after the Allies had landed in Normandy that there occurred the most spectacular political event since 1934 (the Roehm Purge): the Generals' Plot of the 20th of July, 1944, which showed that the leaders of the German Army regarded the War as lost, and were at last prepared to break their alliance with the Party.

The importance of this plot 'cannot be over-rated', says Trevor-Roper: 'After long preparation a small section of the German people had at last taken the initiative.' This section was mainly composed of members of the aristocracy of Eastern Germany (the blow itself was struck in East Prussia), which used to rule the German Army, and now controlled the General Staff. 'Ignoring or over-riding the fumblings and hesitations of more timorous conspirators, it made a positive, determined and nearly successful effort to destroy the Nazi régime.'

Who were these determined conspirators? Some of the

chief names were these: Beck, Treschkow, Witzleben and Stauffenberg.

These men, and some other officers of the General Staff, formed an extremist group among the opponents of the Hitler government. They were not necessarily supported by the other resistance groups. Had they been successful, doubtless the other groups would have joined them, but 'failure frightened them back into mutual distrust and hostility'. The important civilian group led by Goerdeler and Adam von Trott zu Solz seems to have been separate from the Army Group, which was itself subdivided. Thus there was no one unified purpose to weld all these opposition groups into a strong movement. This lack of cohesion was mainly due to the situation in which these men and women had to work. The activities of the Secret Police, and the widespread spying that riddled German life under the Nazis, made any kind of continuous and effective contact and co-operation practically impossible. Separatist planning was inevitable, with all the weakness that this means in a dangerous political situation.

.   .   .   .

The 20th July Plot was well planned, and it nearly succeeded. Several times already the explosive charge had been sent to Hitler's Headquarters, only to be returned unused owing to some technical hitch. Finally, Stauffenberg, when summoned to the H.Q. in East Pussia for consultation with Hitler on military matters, brought the bomb into the wooden hut, concealed in his brief-case. Several other men were present for this conference; Hitler took his seat at the head of the table and the conference began. After a short time Stauffenberg put his brief-case down against the leg of the table and made an excuse to slip out of the room for a moment. Instead of returning to the room Stauffenberg went directly to the plane which he had ordered to be kept in readiness. He was waiting to hear the explosion, so the plane took off and the pilot circled round over the camp, waiting for the bomb to explode. Hitler, hearing a plane overhead, went to the window to see what was happening. Just then the bomb exploded. Hitler was blown through the window and out into the yard. Stauffenberg saw bodies lying outside, and soon others were carried out. He at once flew off to Berlin with the news of Hitler's death. But the news came through immediately (on the private line from Hitler to Goebbels) that Hitler was alive and not much hurt. The plot had failed.

There was great commotion at Rastenburg that day. Mussolini arrived early in the afternoon on a long-expected visit. Hitler was on the platform to meet him, looking as white as a sheet. He told him of his marvellous escape and showed him the smoking débris of the partially ruined hut. At five o'clock there was a tea-party attended by the members of the Hitler 'court'. At first the 'courtiers' wrangled among themselves while Hitler and Mussolini watched them rather grimly. Quite suddenly, someone happened to mention the Roehm plot of June 1934 and the 'bloody purge' which followed it. To Hitler this acted like a match to some highly inflammable material. He jumped up, foaming at the mouth, in a sort of frenzy; for half an hour he screamed and ranted, while the 'courtiers' watched him silently. Visitors were there who thought he had gone mad: 'I don't know,' said one of them later, 'why I didn't go over to the Allies there and then.' Mussolini was embarrassed. Graziani tried to divert people's attention. And all the time men-servants dressed in white were moving about among the company, handing cakes and filling up the tea-cups. Then Hitler went to the telephone and shouted orders to Berlin. This was the signal for everyone to begin to talk at once and there was a general hubbub.

After a few moments Hitler came back and sat down,

sucking brightly coloured pastilles. He was silent now, save that now and again he would murmur some savage phrase about 'blood' or 'Providence' or 'concentration camps'.

In the great 'purge' which followed the *20th July* (which was even more drastic than that of 1934) over fifty officers of the General Staff were executed; some say that about three thousand people were put to death at this time; and many more were imprisoned.

Stauffenberg and three others were shot on the 20th July.

Rommel was given a revolver and a poison capsule; he took the hint and killed himself.

Hitler withdrew into a long period of retirement. Himmler seemed to be successful, but his power began to wane. Hitler became a physical wreck, partly owing to his way of living; partly because his doctors were slowly poisoning him. Meanwhile the war situation was getting worse and the situation inside Germany was deteriorating. Hitler now knew that the Army was against him, especially the officers, so he surrounded himself with Naval and Air Force officers. The only two he trusted were 'toadies' like Keitel and Burgdorf. At his last full-dress conference with his Military Staff he accused the generals to their faces of deceiving him. More and more Hitler's Headquarters degenerated from a War Cabinet into an 'oriental court of flatterers and toadies'.

The wave of arrests which followed the failure of the July Plot swept into the hands of the Gestapo not only people who had supported the conspirators but many others who were known to be opposed to the Hitler régime, though their outward behaviour was 'politically' correct. Everywhere the Nazis smelt 'treachery', all barriers were down and the Gestapo hunted people down quite ruthlessly. Thousands were swept off to prison or concentration camp.

Of the leaders, the military group suffered swiftly, as we have seen. Goerdeler was in prison for months, and when his friends met him again they scarcely knew him. The son of a fellow-prisoner (himself one who abhorred violence and murder) said that when his father met Goerdeler in prison, although they had been close friends for years there was no flicker of recognition; his eyes looked 'dead'; indeed he seemed to be like a dead man who could still walk and speak. Tonelessly and apathetically, when questioned by the Gestapo, he 'denounced' his friends by name and in their presence. His friends believe that he was no coward nor was he disloyal, but that he had been subjected to such psychological torment, and had also received certain injections, that he was no longer responsible for his words or his actions.

Some survivors of these tragic happenings in Germany think that it was not merely the accident of Hitler's escape from death which caused the plot to fail. They believe that the final attempt was already too late. The whole thing had been discussed and considered for too long. Too many persons were involved; and the people as a whole were not able to rise and follow such a lead even if it had been successful; they were too much shaken by air raids and terrorized by Hitler. Yet, says one of them, the attempt had to be made, to save the honour of Germany, and to show that even in Hitler-Germany there were people who valued honour more than life.

O.W.

THE AUTHOR TO THE READER

SHOULD you happen to light upon this book, as it were by chance, perhaps you will dip into it here and there, and then turn away saying: 'This book speaks of things which should not be said in public at all.' No one would agree with you more heartily than I myself! For this book is not an attempt to estimate the most recent historical events in our country from the point of view of the historian, nor do I intend to add to the sum of historical research; nor is this book of sufficient importance to justify its publication as a biographical work, for thousands of other people have passed through similar experiences, and countless persons have suffered far more. Nor is it my aim to have a share in the sorry business of increasing hatred in the world. This small book is simply a record; its aim is to give a true account of facts, without indulging in heroics, or trying to dramatize an experience; it has therefore as little to do with publicity as I myself.

But I must say to those who are going to read this book: there are certain people to whom I *owe* this record of personal experiences. Although I have no desire to expose my personal experience to the public gaze, yet I am anxious to dedicate this work to the following people:

TO MY WIFE
For her incomparable courage
And her unshaken calmness,
Qualities which are only possible
Where the Christian Faith is in control;

TO MY AGED FATHER
In loving respect and gratitude;

TO MY OLD BISHOP
Because when I was in prison
He came unto me, thus fulfilling
The Lord's words in Matthew 25.36;

TO MY CHILDREN
Because, bravely and silently, they helped me
To carry my burden, which, to a greater extent
Than I knew at the time, was their burden too.

TO ALL QUIET, COURAGEOUS CHRISTIAN MEN AND WOMEN
In Berlin and elsewhere, who strengthened me with their
     prayers,
And refreshed me during my imprisonment with their gifts:

TO THOSE GROUPS OF CHRISTIAN PEOPLE, IN GERMANY
AND ABROAD
Who regularly made intercession for me;

AND TO THOSE SERVANTS OF GOD
Who ministered to me in a special way
And helped me to prepare for either: Life or death;
For I shall think of them all with gratitude as long as I live.

And those who—in the providence and wisdom of God—
were called to lay down their lives during this time of trial,
and who praised God by the manner of their death: their
confidence and courage, I would remember in the words
of the Book of Wisdom (3.1-6):

But the souls of the righteous are in the hand of God,
     and there shall no torment touch them.
In the sight of the unwise they seemed to die: and their
     departure is taken for misery,

And their going from us to be utter destruction:

But they are in peace.

For though they be punished in the sight of men, yet is their hope full of immortality.

And, having been a little chastised, they shall be greatly rewarded:

For God proved them, and found them worthy for Himself.

As gold in the furnace hath He tried them, and received them as a burnt offering.

I

INTO THE DARKNESS

ON the 19th of August 1944, at four o'clock in the morning, I left Burg Bodenstein in Eichsfeld, where I had spent the night, and began walking downhill into the valley, in order to catch the early train to Berlin. It was still quite dark, and the stars were shining in the clear sky. The road, which sloped steeply into the valley, was bordered by tall fir trees, which stood out very dark and black against the night sky. Walking downhill in this freshness before the dawn was very pleasant, and I strode along as light-hearted and carefree as any character in one of Eichendorff's Tales.

When I reached the bottom of the valley, the high road turned towards the east, and I looked up into the starlit sky. Suddenly, I had a shock: in the night sky, already touched by the first pale rays of dawn, Orion was shining in all its glory. I had forgotten that at this time of year, when we are already moving unconsciously towards winter, it was possible to see this constellation in the early morning sky—hence this wintry picture of the stars in the middle of summer came upon me quite unexpectedly; and as I gazed at it a profound sense of foreboding seized me, like a sudden pain, and I asked myself: 'What will the coming winter be like, when Orion will be shining in all its glory, above our country in its struggles and sufferings?' Then I began to think: 'And what will the new year of life mean for me, myself, personally?' For this was the day before my forty-fifth birthday, and I had cherished some very pleasant dreams of celebrating the day—in spite of the War

—very quietly, but with a certain festal quality. At this moment, although I am particularly fond of August, as the zenith of the year, I could not help feeling oppressed by a premonition of 'things to come'.

The morning dawned; the air was cool and quiet. There were very few people on the train, and they all looked rather chilly. Later on the sun came out, and the day became warmer. At Barby railway station we had an air alarm, which was nothing unusual. The sirens wailed; the red flags were hung out; the train was emptied; and as we looked up into the sky we saw the great silver birds—so menacing and so brilliant—flying in droves through the glorious blue of the cloudless summer sky, eastwards, towards Berlin.

Then followed a tiresome time of waiting and uncertainty, very trying to the nerves; at last we began to move, very slowly; finally, some hours late, we reached Berlin. I was anxious to see whether my house was still standing. I was relieved to find it had not been touched, and I breathed a sigh of relief when I entered the hall; it was so cool and restful. Our faithful Magdalena had kept dinner for me, but I told her to leave me and serve the meal in the evening; I needed sleep more than anything else, in order to make up for the hours I had lost during the night.

It must have been about four o'clock in the afternoon when suddenly there was a violent and repeated ringing of the bell. As the door was not opened, I realized that Magdalena had not come back from her shopping, so I got up to open the door. Two men were standing on the steps. In a flash I knew what it meant. They did not need to tell me that they belonged to the Gestapo, and that they had come to search the house. I took this almost for granted, and politely asked them in. But the deep sense of repulsion, aroused by such men, made me feel I could not resist saying, ironically: 'And what can I do for you?' This was, of course, quite superfluous, because anyone could see what they were after, by the look in their faces and by their behaviour; in a strange way I seemed to feel I had seen them somewhere before; possibly they had already 'shadowed' me when I was giving lectures and addresses in halls and churches.

Later on, when I was being interrogated, I was reproached for the fact that I received these two men so quietly, as though I had long been prepared to see them; this was, in fact, actually true. Inwardly, I had been prepared for this event for a very long time, and wonderingly, I seemed to hear a voice within me beginning to whisper: 'Now, it's begun!'

The two men searched the house, with a curious mixture of extreme care and great carelessness; I began to wonder whether these excellent Gestapo officials were only thinking of getting through their job as quickly as possible on their free Saturday afternoon, or whether they simply wanted to create a general impression of the degree to which I was dangerous to the State; for they only looked through my possessions in an unsystematic way: now flicking through a pile of letters, then picking out a few books and turning them over; in the cellar they turned over some of my stores of paper, yet they didn't make a thorough search of all my documents. 'After all,' I thought, 'are they only searching the house as a pretext for something else?' It soon became clear to me that this last idea was the right one, for after about half an hour they turned to me and said: 'You are under arrest.' I asked them to show me their warrant. There are no difficulties for the Gestapo. They at once produced a warrant. When I pointed out that the next day was Sunday; that I was engaged to conduct a service, and that if I did not turn up there would be a good deal of difficulty and commotion—they simply brushed my objections aside, saying brusquely: 'We can prevent any commotion!', to which I replied, 'You will not be able to prevent it!' The telephone then began to ring, repeatedly. I was allowed to answer it, but was forbidden to say that I was under arrest. Most of the calls were about the service next day: 'Will you be preaching to-morrow morning?' To each I replied, 'I am sorry, but it is impossible!' A few moments later a particular friend of mine, who was passing through Berlin, rang me up to say that he was in town. 'Come and share a good bottle of wine with me!' to which I replied, with grim humour, 'It's a fine idea . . . but I fear we must postpone it to a later date!' All this time the two men were sitting there like watch-dogs, observing every movement and every word. It was evident that some of my ironical remarks did not please them—at all!

Then I began to get ready to leave. I chose an old suit, but one that was still in fairly good condition; as it was black and well cut, I thought that during judicial examinations, and on other public occasions, it would give me something of a clerical air; later on, I did find that this was a help. In addition to my night things I put in two or three of my last good cigars (in the evening the S.S. Officer who relieved me of all my personal possessions was delighted with them!) In addition to the Bible I took a beautifully bound copy of Von Soden's Greek Testament, because its clear type would make it easy to read in a prison cell. I also put in a light overcoat, and after some cogitation I added a hat. But one difficulty still remained. In my coat pocket there was a short English letter from Robert Mackie, the General Secretary of the World's Student Christian Federation, in his own handwriting. It was only a simple, Christian, brotherly greeting, and neither Robert nor I had previously shown any signs of a gift for political intrigue! But since the Gestapo was always inclined to distrust everyone, they *might* take exception to this letter if they found it; also, I didn't want them to learn from *me* that Schönfeld,[1] and some other friends, were in the habit of bringing greetings of this kind into Germany. I got over this difficulty quite nicely however, by a simple stratagem: by asking a very ordinary question I managed to separate the two men for a few moments; one went into the kitchen, as I wanted him to do, and the other went out for a moment on to the terrace. In a flash, while they were out of the way, I tore up the letter and threw it into a rubbish bucket; then I committed it to Providence to arrange that it would soon become unreadable! This must have taken place, for I never heard any more about it. I still had to wait for Magdalena to come back from her shopping. In less than a quarter of an hour she was there; in spite of the fact that she was only sixteen, she took the news of my arrest as splendidly and as calmly as she had endured the countless air attacks night after night. Then we left the house.

I asked the two gentlemen where we were going. They replied: 'We are acting on instructions from a very high authority.' In the mouth of the Gestapo this could only mean Himmler himself. When the car turned into the Lehrter Strasse and approached the great gates of the prison, my eyes fell on the words over the door—'Headquarters of the National Security Service'. This showed me that I was regarded as a very dangerous political prisoner. As we drove into the courtyard I can still remember how deeply I felt the contrast between the radiant August afternoon and the dirty prison walls.

The initial ceremonies were quite tolerable. I was taken into a small office. The clock on the wall showed that it was a little after five. There were a good many S.S. officers about, of different ranks. I couldn't distinguish them very

[1] Dr. Hans Schönfeld, at that time Director of the Study Department of the World Council of Churches, in Geneva—now at the Ecumenical Centre in Frankfurt.

clearly from one another. One made a record of my personal belongings. The fact that I was a clergyman certainly aroused a great deal of attention, but when they asked me how I had managed to get arrested, I couldn't tell them. Then they took away from me—as from every prisoner—everything with which I could do myself harm: my braces, my tie, my belt, because one might hang oneself with it. I was allowed to keep my shaving tackle, but without the blades, because they might be used to cut an artery. Even my innocent sock-suspenders had to disappear, and I wondered what harm they could do! Even my shoe-laces had to be removed, and if I had not been wearing a sports shirt, I would have had to submit to the indignity (which every well-dressed man would feel) of going about without a collar, and a shirt only fastened with a tiny button. But there was worse to come. I had to give up all my papers and documents, money and articles of value, my gold seal ring, and my good Swiss wrist-watch, my fountain pen, my silver pencil, and finally my wedding ring. I never saw any of these things again.

The worst of all was that I had to give up my Bible and my New Testament. I did protest, but it was no use. Even when I said that I was a clergyman, and that usually the Gestapo had allowed my other friends in the ministry to keep their Bibles, and that the next day was my forty-fifth birthday, and that I wanted to read a Psalm, all they said was: 'This has nothing to do with us!' Finally the official gave me my 'room number'.

At last we reached the point at which I could be taken to my cell. I learned that someone who has been arrested must wait with his face to the wall, and must never look round, or he will be severely punished. I learned that in the prison of the National Security Service the guards were very fond of shouting loud, clear orders in a singularly brutal tone of voice. A little dark man, a miserable speci-

men of the Germanic race, was standing there in his shirt
sleeves without a uniform. It was his work to keep on
calling out numbers in the great hall. When I appeared he
called out: 'Guard No. 3, Entrance 176!' I was shouted
at by an S.S. man, who spoke a most curious German,
taken upstairs into the third storey, and put in cell 176.
Another S.S. man, who spoke an equally peculiar German,
received me, and in a few moments the heavy iron door of
cell 176 was locked behind me.

This was the hardest moment of all, harder than all the
hours and days when death seemed very near. When the
door of the cell was locked I threw myself upon my camp-
bed and prayed, 'Help me to forget this door!'—this
door which had just been locked behind me with such a
sinister, irrevocable sound. This door was quite smooth,
so smooth that even the most ignorant person could understand: 'It's all up! You can't do anything about it!'
There was a little spy-hole in the middle of the door, through
which the guard could look in and see what the prisoner
was doing; above it there was an opening in the wall, in
order that the guard could hear immediately if the prisoner
'got up to any nonsense'. This had the doubtful advantage
that the prisoner himself could hear every sound which
echoed in this great hall. On that particular day, obviously,
a great deal was going on. The little dark man was always
calling out noisily: 'Guard No 3! Entrance so-and-so!'
The Gestapo Prison in the Prinz Albrecht Strasse had long
been filled to overflowing; here in the Lehrter Strasse two
wings of the building had already been set apart as a
prison for the Ministry of National Security.

I realized at once that nothing could happen before Mon-
day, that everything was over for the day. Even the meagre
'supper' had already been doled out; I began to feel very
hungry, for I had been on the go since three o'clock in the
morning, and had missed my dinner. However, a bit of

dry bread was brought to me by one of my fellow-prisoners, and there was water in the jug in my cell. The jug, the wash-basin, the plate and spoon, were all terribly worn and dirty; as for the sheets and blankets on the bed, they made me feel quite sick.

Like most people in a similar position I was at first quite cheerful, and was sure I'd 'only be here for a few days!' But when I looked out of the window, and saw the tops of some tall trees rising in their majesty above the high walls, their dark green foliage standing out against the cloudless blue of the August sky, suddenly—just as I felt very early that morning—I had an inexplicable feeling that possibly I would still be here when these trees were yellow and bare. It was a depressing thought. I felt as if someone had struck me.

Then fear and panic began to creep over me, like an evil beast creeping out of its den. I began to see myself and my position very clearly. The dirty cell, with its iron bars— while the blue vault of the cloudless summer sky outside scarcely seemed real any longer. I felt myself enclosed by an invisible wall, the wall of the dark and dangerous and menacing present, against which an individual is outwardly defenceless. I realized that I might 'disappear' within this prison, and that no one would ever know what had become of me.

The more I reflected on the details of my situation, the tighter was the grip of fear. Slowly it began to dawn on me that those dark spots on the floor were not due to dirt, but to blood, which no amount of scrubbing would remove. That dark patch by the bed must have been caused by some unfortunate person who had cut his arteries; then I looked towards the window, and saw another large dark patch, and realized that this must be due to someone who had tried to commit suicide on that spot.

Then, as my ears began to get accustomed to the noises outside in the great hall of this wing of the prison, I began to distinguish all kinds of sounds. The acoustics were like those of a great church hall, but since all the staircases and corridors were made of iron, and there was no wood which would have toned down the noise, every sound was very harsh, and seemed very near. Through the opening above the cell door I was battered by noise, a noise which never ceased. As I listened, I heard some more cell numbers being called out. I wondered what this meant. Were new prisoners being admitted or were men being released, or were they going to be interrogated, ill-treated, or even worse? I couldn't tell.

Now I began to realize that in the next cell I could clearly hear a terrible groaning, sometimes loud and sometimes feeble, broken now and again by feeble cries, and each time the guard came to the door, and looked at my unknown neighbour, while I wondered whether the poor man was ill, or whether he had been tortured. These groans and whimpering complaints of my unknown fellow-prisoner impressed me very painfully; more than his physical suffering, I felt the loss of human dignity expressed in these terrible sounds. Then, a few cells further along, on the left, a prisoner went mad, and kept on banging against his door, crying out: 'I am innocent! I am innocent!' showing that he had wholly lost all self-control. I could hear everything that went on, I even heard when he was given an injection, which was followed by a sinister quietness.

At this moment I made a resolve. I determined to mobilize all my faculties of spiritual and mental resistance, in order that under no circumstances should I break down like this.

At last, one of the most precious gifts was granted me—which has been of priceless value to me throughout my life—the gift of sleep. I laid myself down on the plank bed to sleep; I was needing it very badly, for I had had a very long, eventful day. So in spite of the hard bed, and the incessant noise, and even in spite of the horrible, brilliant lamp which glared down upon us all night long, I slept in peace and quietness; when I woke up next morning, I felt greatly refreshed and strengthened; and everything looked different.

It was Sunday, the 20th of August, 1944—my forty-fifth birthday: a day of radiant sunshine, just the kind of weather I had hoped to have at this time of year. 'Broad August' was shining in a dazzling vault of light, and the earth was bathed in glowing heat. Suddenly, from a window in another wing, I heard someone whistling the first line of a familiar hymn. I was electrified, sprang to the window, and as soon as my unknown companion ceased whistling I answered with the chorale: 'Oh for a thousand tongues to sing . . .' We went on whistling like this, antiphonally, until the guard at the end of the corridor made a sudden noise; we stopped instantly; when the guard in my own corridor came along to see what was happening I was lying peacefully upon my bed, and he went away, none the wiser!

Once more, for a moment, that gradual sense of panic, which had gripped me the previous evening, began to invade my mind. I had just heard some shots, close at hand: they were so regular that at first I actually thought that the S.S. men were simply practising shooting, when, suddenly, the idea occurred to me that people in our prison were now being 'liquidated'.

Then, over the roofs floated the sound of distant bells. I tried to guess the time by the position of the sun; hour after hour I lived through this Sunday morning: picturing the waiting congregation, and in spirit I held the service with my people. Just then I put my hand in my pocket, and found a scrap of crumpled paper which I had not noticed, nor had it been discovered by the official who had searched me. It contained some notes for my sermon on 1 Corinthians 15.1-10, on which I had meant to preach; now I was able to think over the text once more.

During the first few days I didn't see anything of my fellow-prisoners. The cell numbers, which were continually being called out in those early days, concealed the identity of everyone in an oppressive kind of anonymity. On the fourth or fifth day, however, a group of us was photographed for the criminal register. We stood upon the staircase, and in the corridors, at long distances from one another, with our faces to the wall, until we were called to go outside to be photographed. The photograph itself was extremely badly done, and since it was not at all clear, to avoid further errors, our names were called out; in this way I learned that my neighbour was called Schulenburg. Then I heard other names, which all pointed in the same direction. I then began to understand that I was considered to have some connection with the events of the 20th of July. While we were being photographed I realized that if you take a face that has not been shaved, and add to it the fact that the man has no collar, it is extremely easy to turn a quite honest face into that of a criminal, especially when the victim is told that he must look *down*; since I did not know what publicity might be given to this picture, I held my head up, and looked up at the sun, in order that I might cut a good figure in the photograph, for once my face had been photographed, there it would stay. However, the second time the photograph was taken, one of the S.S. officials saw what I was doing, and he shouted at me: 'Chin well *down*!' Evidently I don't belong to that group of human beings who are allowed to pose as a hero!

One good thing came out of this brief encounter with my fellow-prisoners. My mind had been churning over and over the question: 'Why have I been arrested?' Now my thoughts were turned in another direction. Until then I thought there were three different possibilities. The first concerned Gerstenmaier. He had been arrested on the evening of the 20th of July, at the Army Headquarters, with York and others. Although I knew no details, of course I knew of his ecumenical contacts. He had made it possible for Schönfeld and others to keep in touch with the various ecumenical bodies in Geneva; in this way we had regularly received news from various foreign churches. I had kept in touch with new books in theology, and had sometimes received greetings from foreign friends. Now all this was very far from making me a danger to the State; for every Christian, and indeed for every reasonable man, it was quite clear that all this had nothing to do with 'politics'; but of course I did realize that these 'international' contacts looked very suspicious to the Gestapo. Thus whatever Christian or Church resistance already existed in Germany seemed doubly suspect when it was reinforced from the world outside; further, the untravelled German disliked all that was 'foreign'; hence it was evident that public opinion would regard any proceedings against us as absolutely justified, for the reasons mentioned. Now Frau Gerstenmaier, whom I had seen several times, told me that the Gestapo were hunting for a secret document which her husband was supposed to have in his possession. There had been trouble about this before, and I had already received a warning about it, but since I did not possess any such document I had not paid much attention to these warnings. At the same time I was not wholly unprepared.

The second possibility was connected with Goerdeler. After a lecture which I had given in a church in Leipzig, on the 'Possibilities of a Christian Life in the Present Situation', he came to me in the vestry, and tried to 'sound' me. The unusual frankness with which Goerdeler had talked about his plans had already aroused my distrust. His outspokenness was doubtless due to his personal fearlessness;

but since he had no hesitation in talking freely about his plans over the telephone to a large number of people whom I knew, his behaviour seemed to me both strange and irresponsible. I still cannot understand why it was, that, in view of all this frankness and carelessness on the part of people who were not even sworn conspirators the Gestapo did not discover the persons who were mainly involved in the conspiracy, nor were they able to forestall the events of the 20th of July. All I can conclude is: either that there were too many conspirators in the ranks of the Gestapo itself—and, if so, this could only mean that their own leaders were involved—or, the Gestapo was less competent than the ordinary German citizen believed. Probably both these guesses are not far from the truth. In the later weeks of my imprisonment I saw more than one S.S. leader under arrest, who had been in some way involved in the events of the 20th of July. On the other hand, I told one of the Gestapo officials who was examining me, that, so far as I was concerned, I could not understand why, in midsummer 1944, the Gestapo were still busy examining clergy from the Berlin Confessional Church, in order to find out where they sent the money which they collected, while almost under their eyes a conspiracy against Hitler's very life was being prepared.

To return to Goerdeler—I treated him with reserve, because I did not feel myself called to take immediate or direct political action. At that time I had such a flourishing activity in the form of lectures and public meetings, that even now I look back with emotion on that period, so full of tension and expectancy, when under the increasingly heavy attacks from the air people's spiritual hunger became more and more evident. Even now I can recall the picture of those crowded churches—often with congregations of from two to three thousand people. To-day most of those churches are in ruins. I could not doubt that *this* was my real work, and since I was a preacher of the Gospel, I had no right to wish to be anything else.

But I was very near the circle of those who were working against Hitler. They often frequented the churches where I was preaching, and at that time a certain circle of people in Germany knew each other, and were sure of each other, without further ado. Thus I took no active share in the preparations for the events of the 20th of July, and my acquaintances (who respected my spiritual calling, without saying a word about it) never asked me to take an active part. Yet as a matter of course I was present at many conversations about the future, where the Church and the spiritual life of our people were concerned. At that time, however, if anyone was clear how all this would end—and I had no longer the slightest doubt that we were heading for catastrophe—then it would have been treachery to one's own country *not* to think about the future. But it is evident that all this did not constitute an 'active share' in the preparations for the 20th of July.

Goerdeler's view of this *coup d'état* seems to have been different from that of Stauffenberg, but later on, when Goerdeler was in flight, and came to see me, asking for my advice, I helped him, as the Church had so often done in earlier days. Later on I admitted this fact to the Gestapo.

My third supposition was more general in character. From the standpoint of the Gestapo, I had long been a marked man. For some time past, all kinds of things had been happening to me: sometimes I was banished from a district, or I would be forbidden to speak for a certain space of time, or my passport would be taken from me; then I was forbidden to publish my newspaper; I was often interrogated. In short, these were all 'warnings'—warnings which fell to the lot of many honest Germans who could not wholly avoid playing some part in public life. Finally, the Gestapo showed me what they really thought about me when, a few days before the 20th of July, they forbade me to travel about at all; this meant that, apart from my preaching in Berlin, I was also prevented from speaking. Thus, apart from the events of the 20th of July, in their eyes I was already a marked man. From *their* point of view, of course, they had every reason for suspicion. From the standpoint of real law and justice, of course, I was innocent; but if the reason for my arrest was my hostility to the fundamental doctrines of National Socialism, which was evident in all my public activity, then there was no point in considering the possibilities from the point of view of law; from the moment I was arrested the authorities showed quite plainly that they had no idea of acting according to law, for they neither gave me a reason for my arrest, nor the possibility of a proper trial; they simply left me alone in my cell, in spite of the fact that every day I asked for legal aid. I had slowly made up my mind that I must be prepared for every eventuality, however sinister.

At first, it seemed to me that the saddest, and the most depressing group of men in our prison were our guards. They were S.S. Germans from Roumania and various Balkan countries; most of them were still very young; some were only eighteen or nineteen years old. Their German was very defective, and some could only speak broken German. I had to listen to them yelling at me in the most extraordinary lingo! In spite of the noise they made, they really were rather comic, and this gave me some private amusement! Sometimes, to the extreme astonishment of these young men, I yelled back at them, which they certainly didn't expect!

They had been withdrawn from the Front for the sole purpose of acting as jailers to 'traitors'. It had been dinned into them that they must not treat these 'traitors' gently, and they did their best to carry out these orders as literally as possible; with most of these young soldiers the fact of being 'drest in a little brief authority', and allowed to order generals and professors about, went to their heads! This meant that they were able to give vent to their repressions and their sense of inferiority.

When I looked at the faces of my fellow-prisoners, bearing deep traces of sorrow and suffering, the faces of people who in ordinary life had been used to holding positions of great responsibility, and when I saw the dignity with which they bore their fate, I could never get rid of the impression that it was all an uncanny muddle! It was as if the rôles played by these people had been changed by malicious demons, for in point of fact prisoners and guards ought to have changed places, or so it seemed—or was this whole situation only the symbolic development of a political order which was on the verge of collapse?

Later on, when I learned to distinguish the faces of these men better, I changed my opinion completely. It was a long time before this happened, however, because during the early weeks of my imprisonment I was not allowed to speak to a soul (for many weeks I lived like a Trappist); also, the guards were continually changed, in order that there might be no suspicion of any familiarity between the prisoners and their guards; so that it was a long while before the veil of impersonality, in which our guards were enveloped, was lifted. In spite of this, gradually I began to distinguish the faces of those who had some goodness of disposition left, who, under their hardened outward bearing, had preserved some humanity, and with whom one could get into contact. In time, however, I learned to have a quite different opinion even of the younger ruffians, for in a very special way they were victims of the Third Reich. When they were very young, without any real knowledge of the actual character of the Third Reich, when the German troops marched into their country, they had been persuaded or urged to join the S.S. Most of them had not seen their relatives for a very long time, and now that the Russian troops had marched into their countries, they were usually very anxious about their families. Long ago they had lost the moral protection of their home country. The S.S. atmosphere in sex matters had done its work with them, and now these young, healthy, vigorous men, capable of bearing arms, had been ordered back to Berlin, simply to do the work of prison guards. Literally, their whole life consisted in this extremely monotonous duty: four hours on guard, four hours fatigue-duty, four hours off. In their own time they were left quite free to do what they liked and as I listened to their loud, outspoken conversations I realized the kind of 'pleasures' they sought and enjoyed in ruined Berlin. Most of them simply went to pieces, and this not even in a very dramatic way, simply because they had nothing to do; the emptiness of their life, and the fact that they were forced to be brutal, caused them to crumble inwardly. As I watched these young faces, and saw them becoming increasingly dull and vacant, it was difficult to discover any traces of the fresh and honest peasant boys of other days! It is painful to reflect that the Third Reich took as many victims from their ranks as from ours. Most of their N.C.O.s were worthless people. How foolish many of them were came out very clearly when, towards the end, when the ultimate outcome could no longer be in doubt, they tried to conserve the existing 'order' with redoubled brutality—although so far as we were concerned, this 'order' was not menaced by us—largely for prudential reasons!

Later on, however, I was able to get into touch with one and another of these young men, and I had serious conversations with some of them. I simply could not look on, and see these young men being wasted like this, and say nothing at all about it. It was quite simple to get into touch with them. In our usual daily contacts with our guards, like putting our water-jugs outside the cell, or in taking our clean towels from them, I would simply say 'Thank you', not with any special emphasis, but as one does if one is well brought up. It was quite astonishing to see how differently various men reacted to these simple little words. In any case it often opened up the way for me to make contact with those who desired it, and sometimes gave me an opportunity for serious conversation.

Once I completely upset the equilibrium of an old, dried-up official by using this word. This happened in Tegel, and it was during the first difficult days in Tegel when the order to be chained was still quite new. One evening this old man had to fasten my fetters before I went to sleep; when he had finished I couldn't resist saying to him, in a very polite and courteous voice, 'Thank you very much'. He stood still and stared at me; then he went out of the cell; and in a moment or two he came back again, and said in an awkward, rough voice: 'No need to thank me for a thing like that!' I replied: 'Well, you have only done your duty!'—an expression dear to the heart of any good German official! If he had not lost the power of expressing emotion and tenderness, he would have done so now, but this was beyond him, so shaking his head he strode out of the room, murmuring to himself.

And so the time passed, in darkness and uncertainty. My solitude was complete; apart from the few necessary words exchanged between me and my guards I was completely silent. Each morning, at midday, and in the evening, meals were brought to me; this was all the contact between my cell and the outside world. I had no watch; I hadn't a scrap of paper for writing or reading; only the four bare walls of the cell; that was all. I realized that I must gather up all my mental and spiritual forces, in order not to go to pieces; I had no contact with the outside world at all.

And yet the consolation of God did not fail. One of His lesser consolations was the fact that one day when I was looking out of my window I saw a falcon flying round in the sky. The sky was absolutely cloudless, and the sun shone down into the grey bare quadrangle of the prison courtyard, which seemed devastatingly empty under the summer sky. Suddenly, the falcon rose into the light blue above us and wheeled around with his glorious wings— a wonderful picture of freedom. There was nothing in this empty prison courtyard to attract him, so far as I could see, so I had the impression that God had sent him; and the words of Calvin on the 104th Psalm flashed into my mind with a deep sense of consolation: 'Status mundi in dei laetitia fundatus est.' When the supernatural world is a present reality and more powerful than that of our external world, then even the smallest ray of its glory illumines our path, and lights up our life with a ray of eternal significance.

I shall never forget the first day we were allowed to have a short walk in the open air. I can still feel it. It was one of those lovely days in October, full of the transparent clarity of a glorious autumn, which I love more than any other time of year. It was in Tegel, where the very rigid but regular routine of the day was controlled by the Prussian Judicial administration. Since no one had forbidden it, in accordance with the prison routine we were turned out early into the courtyard for a walk. The weather was almost as warm as summer. Above the high walls I saw the first pale gold of a birch tree and it was extraordinarily sweet to breathe the air, this pure autumnal air. I literally drank it in while I sought in vain to remember the great passages in our classical poetry where the air of freedom is sung. But I couldn't remember them so I turned to the praises of the Psalms. After so many weeks of confinement this moment still stands out in my memory as something I can never forget.

II

UNDER CROSS-EXAMINATION

I ENTERED the most difficult period of my imprisonment under the Gestapo in a buoyant spirit of what might be called a 'private optimism'; literally, in the first few moments, this 'optimism' vanished! For already I felt the scorching breath of an historical sirocco! In a flash my naïve expectation that 'it wouldn't be so bad after all!' was swept away. It was as though I had been living in a fog, in which personal and private considerations were uppermost. Suddenly, the fog lifted, and I saw that I was involved in the whole broad front of an historic resistance to the power of Evil, in its political form.

The Gestapo knew a great deal more about me than I had ever guessed, although they did not know everything. Very slowly it dawned upon me that for a long time past they had honoured me with a great deal of their attention. My arrest was only the climax of a process which had already been foreshadowed by that general prohibition of travel and speaking before the 20th of July. In the eyes of the Gestapo I had long been a marked man.

My arrest seemed to give them the opportunity of 'eliminating' me at once, for it presupposed that I had been deeply implicated in the events of the 20th of July. This very soon became plain to me when, on a beautiful sunny, clear August morning, Dr. Neuhaus began to examine me in the Headquarters of the National Security Service in the Meinekestrasse. Dr. Neuhaus was a very excitable person, dark-haired, of middle height; he was much feared, on account of the way in which he conducted his interrogations. He had managed to condemn to death all the ring-leaders of the 20th of July Plot, especially those who had been arrested first of all. His colleagues regarded him as a man who understood 'these things' better than them all. When I managed to discover his name upon a document or an envelope (otherwise this house was concealed under a terrible veil of impersonality) I saw at once that I was regarded as a very 'dangerous' political prisoner.

But he did not begin at once. At the outset his behaviour to me was absolutely that of a gentleman. I was not fettered; the proceedings took place in a room belonging to the Gestapo, furnished like a club, with comfortable chairs. Even when later on he began to threaten and insult me, still I was not tortured, which was the usual procedure in these rooms, and on such occasions. I was surprised and puzzled by the fact that I was not tortured, not only on this occasion, but on several others, including my trial by Freisler, in the People's Court. After a great deal of thought I can only find one explanation: I have frequently come into contact with 'children of this world' who in the depths of their souls still have a superstitious awe of the office of the clergy; probably my enemies acted as they did from an unconscious desire to show that they were 'not so bad after all'.

But this did not prevent Dr. Neuhaus from displaying the 'glories' of his well-earned reputation. After a few intro-ductory formal remarks of a personal character, the exam-ination began; in a few moments I realized that I was no longer a law-abiding citizen, with whom no one could find anything seriously wrong; I saw plainly that I was on trial for my life. For here there was no attempt to discover the truth of the situation, as exactly and as carefully as possible; here, I was confronted by a man who *willed* my death. This was a new experience for me: to be confronted by a person who was trying to compass my death, by means of a cold,

clear, dispassionate conversation. What a terrible trans-
formation! There was no sharp dagger, no brutal blow,
yet the murderous instrument, which hung over my head
for hours, was a system of questioning, of quite demonic
precision.

The art of Dr. Neuhaus was, in fact, literally *demonic*;
and the slight but noticeable fear which it evoked was
peculiar; we can only understand it if we think that the
devil, with his cunning, is cleverer than we are. Here a
power of active evil was at work, bent on 'breaking' the
accused, both in mind and will, a subtle process of 'head-
hunting', aiming at catching the victim out in his speech,
a method which was much more subtle, and much more
precise in its operations than that of the skill of a great
surgeon with his knife. It was almost impossible to evade
those invisible snares which were cast around one with
every question, each of them fraught with deadly poten-
tiality.

After the first three sentences I realized that these questions were sharply polished daggers each of which was
intended to inflict a deadly wound. I can still recall the
moment when I understood, in a flash, that in this intricate
web of question and answer the exciting and terrible gamble
for life or death had begun.

Still more agitating was the realization that with each
answer I held in my hands not only my own fate but that
of some other human being. In all this conflict I had to
find my way completely in the dark, for I had no exact
news of my closer acquaintances. I did not know whether
Trott and Schulenburg, Schacht and Goerdeler, Gerstenmaier and others were still alive, nor did I know which of
them had been arrested, nor had I any idea what those who
had been arrested (whether they were still alive or not)
might have said. This uncertainty was a torment, for everyone will understand that I did not feel in the least free to

compromise at any point. I could not, and would not make confessions on behalf of others, and I never would have done so.

So far as I myself was concerned, I had a very simple method, which proved to be the right one. I confined myself to answering the questions put to me in the narrowest and most precise sense, but what I said in my answer was completely true. It was quite clear to me that, as a clergyman, and in this sense one who had fallen into the hands of the Gestapo for the sake of the Gospel, I could not have anything to do with lies. But, when my answers involved others, I often found it difficult to act on this principle. The very fact that in such instances I sometimes hesitated before I replied always made my interrogator very angry. The Gestapo, as we can well understand, had no use for such chivalry. Thus in the questions which concerned other people, almost more than in those which affected myself personally, I became aware of the demonic intention of this art of questioning. It was a demonic art, but it was 'demonic' not only because it was conducted with a devastating intelligence, but also because it had, quite unexpectedly, and most fortunately, moments of sheer stupidity! It was an art with a blind spot. In the technique of questioning used by this famous interrogator—so much admired by his colleagues—I began to see that a man whose whole soul is bent on cunning, sometimes cannot even *see* the truth! His extremely astute, almost fool-proof method of examining his prisoners had one quite elementary, but formidable defect—prejudice. Thus he began to "examine' me, taking for granted that I had been involved in this plot against Hitler; at all costs, then, he was determined to extract from my own lips the confession that I knew all about it; this would have been quite enough to justify a sentence of death. It was to this aim that he directed all his interrogation, but for the sake of this aim, he failed to notice quite essential matters which were discussed in the course of the questioning, if they did not seem to him to be related to this final purpose. In the five main examinations to which I had to submit before the People's Court, almost every critical point in my previous career, above all in the later years, was mentioned. Many of them were not even recorded, because, owing to the fact that he was so set upon his deadly aim, he failed at the moment to perceive their significance. Certainly my principles did not lead me to draw his attention to this point!

Further, I seriously believe that this simple method of sticking to the truth served to protect me. Frequently, it gave me a particular kind of assistance. Since I have a good memory, I could make exact statements about times, almost down to a quarter of an hour. I noticed that the police, who were always looking out for the bad element in human beings, were always favourably impressed by such exactness of statement, although I am fully aware that a good memory and the love of truth are two different things. On some points even a tyrant is easily satisfied!

Dr. Neuhaus did not altogether disdain the use of a method common to criminal lawyers of the second rank, that is, the surprise question, which even he would suddenly fire off unexpectedly, like a shot, from the background. (One of these 'shots' showed how gladly he would have caught Dibelius,[1] whom he obviously missed amongst his victims.) He was clever enough to see that I only regarded these surprise questions as 'shots', intended to intimidate; and he did not repeat them. So far as his reputation as a criminal lawyer was concerned, a little scene took place which was rather compromising for him, and of interest to me. During the morning, in the middle of the examination,

[1] Dr. Otto Dibelius, now Lutheran Bishop of Berlin; a fearless opponent of the Nazi Government; Chairman at the present time (1949) of the United Evangelical Church in Germany.

the air-raid alarm sounded. I said that I was quite prepared to remain where we were, and to 'carry on'; at first Dr. Neuhaus pretended to be quite unmoved, but gradually he became more and more nervous; at last he insisted that we should go down to the shelter. As we entered the spacious subterranean refuge, Neuhaus was greeted with joyful cries from some very attractive young women secretaries; to put it mildly, this showed that he enjoyed a considerable popularity. At this moment, of course, this joviality was not very agreeable to him; so we went on into another room, where we were almost in the dark. We sat down upon a simple wooden bench and prepared to carry on in a serious way. He was reading a document, and I sat still and reflected. After a few moments of silence an S.S. standard-bearer came in; he was a little tipsy and very jovial. In the half-light he greeted me with a courteous bow, which I naturally returned; then in rather noisy tones, he asked Neuhaus: 'Well, and who have you got rid of to-day?', when Neuhaus, naturally, made some evasive answers, and tried to shut him up, this man (not realizing the situation at all) cried out, 'Oh! what a hypocrite you are, you know you can do this sort of thing better than all of us!' then he looked at me in a bleary, facetious, uncertain way, for confirmation! After this little scene Neuhaus had to use every art of his famous technique of 'questioning' in order to steer the conversation out of these troubled waters into calmer regions. You will understand why I feel that I cannot omit this little scene!

The concrete result of this first day's interrogation was quite clear. It was established that my relations with the conspirators, though numerous, were purely of a pastoral nature. It is obvious that the Gestapo could not be satisfied with a result of this kind, so they redoubled their efforts to get more out of me, but those who conducted the other interrogations were not of the same calibre as Dr. Neuhaus.

In consequence, their intention to condemn me to death stood out quite plainly, but this made it all the easier to baffle them—so the last two interrogations tried to prove that I had contacts with foreign countries. Naturally, I had many such contacts. Compared with my numerous contacts with churches in other countries the knowledge of the official who was examining me—a dissatisfied, narrow-minded and therefore dangerous pedant—was extremely meagre. He seemed to be impregnated with the widespread notion that all foreign countries were worthless; therefore it surprised him greatly when I freely admitted that I had a great deal of intercourse with foreign countries; I added, however, that these were of an official character, and that for years they had been guaranteed and supported by the Foreign Office. This fact having been established at the beginning of the interrogation, his examination lost its certainty and its edge, and ended very lamely. This was still more true of his last interrogation. Obviously he had been told that under all circumstances he must discover something highly treacherous; somebody must have told him about some certainly very unpleasant expressions of opinion in the Swiss Press, which had appeared in the Press Service of the Evangelical Churches. He then asked me what were my relations with this organization. I had none. He did not want to give up the struggle quite so easily, so he suggested that I was not telling him the truth; I then became vehement, and, with a very superior air—as of one who really knows what he is talking about, I said: ' You gentlemen continually overlook the fact that Switzerland is a Calvinist country; now I am the General Secretary of the Lutheran World Convention, and this body has no official relations with Switzerland, with the exception of two extremely small congregations in Zurich and Basle! ' In order to defend himself he immediately replied: ' Oh, of course I know that '; but he had lost the thread of his argument and could carry it no further, so this last interrogation was finished after a few moments. But this examination left me with a very unpleasant feeling: first of all, it saddened me to know that men of my own race had obviously decided to hound me to death under any pretext that they could find. But I felt more than indignation; I was bewildered. What were they driving at? This 'desire to kill' which was so widespread, far beyond the walls of this prison, was like a madman striking out wildly in every direction; and as I thought about it, I realized how uncertain such a system must be, if it hits out to so little purpose. The two comprehensive examinations which dealt with my activity as a preacher, however, were very different; I had to take them far more seriously than the dangerous attacks of Dr. Neuhaus. In any case, they were both interesting and instructive, for they showed me the picture which the Gestapo had made of the Church and of Christendom— 'You know that you are a most dangerous man,' began my interrogator, after the usual formalities, when I was brought (not in chains) before the Headquarters of the Gestapo in the Französiche Strasse. He was a very different man from Neuhaus; on the whole, he was a remarkable mixture of cleverness and simplicity, humanity and fidelity to Gestapo principles. Thus in the midst of the inquiry he allowed me to have a short telephone conversation with my wife, with whom I had not yet had any contact since my arrest. Obviously he did this against all their principles, on his own responsibility, and the reason for this bold and humane behaviour was easy to perceive. My wife had made a particularly good impression upon him by her calmness and her courage. On the other hand, he did not disdain to use all kinds of threatening and insulting remarks; similarly he could interlard quite intelligent and sensible observations with stupidly naïve remarks. For instance, he once interrupted me to ask: 'When was the Gospel of John written?'

and when I replied, in academic terms, that this was a question that could not be answered without a good deal of discussion, he almost bit off my head, saying, 'In the year 254'. He then began to support this startling statement with a rambling account of the results of his own private reading, obviously of books which he had not thoroughly understood. On the other hand, he *had* understood the depth of the principles on which the Church struggle was conducted, and was able to distinguish between questions of primary and secondary importance. He spoke with contempt of those 'confessors' who for 'the sake of the Gospel' occupied a position from which they refused to budge, and then, perhaps after being arrested or suffering some defeat, were very ready to move. As an example of this he mentioned the question of the theological examinations of the Confessional Church. He did not hold a very high opinion of some members of that Church, who were regarded as pillars, while he spoke with evident respect of the reality of the faith of some other brethren in the Confessional Church, as, for instance, of President Scharf.

He was very critical of the fact that Eva Bildt was my secretary; for a long time it looked as though my great crime was the fact that I had employed a person who, in the language of the Third Reich, was 'half-Aryan'. Actually this point was an extremely troublesome part of the whole interrogation, although there was very little to say. In his mind it was all connected with his main charge against me; for he was sure I knew a great deal about the 20th of July Plot, and at the bottom of his heart he was convinced that I had gone further. He was sure that the 'conspirators and traitors' would not have come to me to such an extent for pastoral help, or looked to me as their clergyman, if I had not given them occasion to believe that without entering into political activity I was one of the most decided spiritual opponents of National Socialism. Here it came out that the Gestapo knew and understood much more of my lecturing activity than my friends had been inclined to believe. This man, in any case, had not been deluded by cleverly worded formulae. And since in my public speeches, I avoided aggressive polemics, at least in the sense of putting them in the foreground, and in general I expressed myself in moderate terms, in his eyes this procedure seemed especially dangerous. Thus it was this man, who, on that particular morning, began with the challenging sentence—'You know that you are a most dangerous man!' Taken aback, I replied, 'Surely not!' He did not understand my reaction, and replied, 'How can you deny it?'

I: 'Because hundreds have been much braver and cleverer than I!'

He: 'Ha! Braver and cleverer? Who then was it who used to speak in the Berlin Confessional Church whenever they wanted to draw large crowds? Who was it who held such large meetings in Leipzig, and Hanover, and Stuttgart, and Heidelberg, and other places? If there had only been forty or even a hundred people there, we wouldn't have said anything, but when *you* spoke there were always thousands of people present! This shows there was something wrong!'

It soon came out that, as he himself said, for the last two years he had followed every detail of my career and my public activity; he only needed to open a drawer of his writing-table with his left hand, while he was talking, and he could produce a copy of almost each of the more important lectures I had given during those years; in some instances his recollection was more exact and more reliable than my own. The conversation soon became one which dealt with principles. I complained bitterly that no public space for activity and public life was granted to us as Christians.

He: 'Why do you continually attack National Socialism?'

I: 'There are fundamental doctrines of National Socialism about which a Christian can never remain silent. Why do you force upon us Christians, in the name of political renewal, such absolutely pagan doctrines like those of the worthlessness of human life? Or why do you suspect us of being enemies of the State when we are simply proclaiming our faith?'

He: 'It is exactly because you have expressed such convictions that you are now here.'

I: 'But you must admit that I have tried hard not to give offence to the authorities?'

He: 'That's just what I mean! You were not so stupid as to occupy yourself with secondary questions, like collections, examinations and similar things, you were always out for the whole! You always went to the heart of things!'

He then took up a copy of my last public lecture, which was entitled, 'Is God Silent?'; he read page after page, picking out sentence after sentence and emphasizing them; every now and again he would stop and say: 'There you are! Another shot, right on the target!' For me it was both unexpected and illuminating to listen to such a direct, official, National Socialist reaction to my lecture. I cannot deny that my remarks suddenly seemed far more clear and pointed than they had sounded when I first wrote the lecture. I had simply tried to preach the Gospel, and to explain some fundamental Christian convictions. If this led to my being regarded as part of the Resistance Movement I couldn't help it; I certainly had not sought either a cheap rhetorical victory, or the glory of a martyr. Now I began to see, to a far greater extent than I had been aware during that period of service, that this activity was part of that great historical Resistance Movement, which I had so suddenly perceived at my first interrogation. In spite of my personal situation and my surroundings, I saw in this an

occasion for great thankfulness, for it confirmed my conviction that I was on the right path. So, after he had attacked
me several times more, I simply said, 'If I am not allowed
to say things like that in the Third Reich, then I am very
glad to be here!' and I left that building with a certain
exaltation of spirit. To me the two Fronts now seemed
clear, and these two examinations had shown me the real
reason for my arrest; this roused in me a sense of gratitude.
I feel I must pay a tribute to that official, because his in-
quiries so often did lead us to points of fundamental principle. When this happened, in spite of all that was repellent
and difficult, I felt that unmistakable attraction and sympathy which even an opponent arouses in us, when the
enmity is clear and outspoken. He himself was evidently
conscious of the contrast between the Christian Faith and
National Socialism, and he saw that it was one which
could be neither evaded nor ignored. If he had been able
to express himself on this subject, I think he would have
admitted that there could be no connection between the
substitute faith of National Socialist fanaticism and that
which the Christian confesses as his faith; that the fanatical
belief of the National Socialist, which was entirely a 'substitute' religion, although nihilistic in tendency, ruled out
the Christian Faith entirely because it could not admit the
force of the First Commandment: 'Thou shalt have none
other gods before me'; in rejecting this commandment it
rejected all the others as well.

In point of fact he was completely immersed in the
National Socialist world of thought. He was quite convinced—in an infantile way—that the clergy had really nothing to do except to preach on Sundays, and when I once
casually mentioned a decree of the Party, which was aimed
against the Church, saying that it was not only politically
unnecessary but simply foolish, he shouted out: 'What's
that? There's only one thing *we* find any use and that is

the clenched fist!' This took place towards the end of the year 1944, it is true, and it was another small pointer, showing the strange decline of a political world which could not even see *itself* any longer in a realistic manner. This was due to the fact that it was full of this fanatical faith, which prevented it from seeing things clearly, just as its propagandists believed that medieval piety was similarly blinded. But the two long interrogations to which he subjected me stand out in my memory as different from the others, although there was of course a certain similarity. So far as I could tell, he seemed to me to act from conviction, and unconsciously he seemed to respect my convictions; for instance, when, in the midst of a conversation, I expressed, very strongly, my sense of responsibility as a preacher, which could not be restricted by any earthly authority, he took it very quietly; and his secretary handed me, as a silent token of recognition, a cigarette. All this softened the impression of something inhuman and evil which otherwise brooded over this institution.

I was particularly grateful for the fact that I was able to go through all these interrogations with the greatest freshness and elasticity. The first one, under Dr. Neuhaus, began early in the morning. That is all I can say, for I had no watch. When, at the end of this day, I was being led back into my cell, my eyes fell upon a clock in the writing-room through which I was passing, it was exactly midnight. All day long I had been engaged in this gruelling examination, with one short pause when I was given a plate of soup; that was all; it was not only the exciting 'give-and-take' of the drama of life and death which had kept me on the alert. I was really tireless, and without wearying I followed all the 'ins and outs' of this game without slackening. The other interrogations, too, did not tire me out. However strange this may seem, I could not have had any better preparation for these cross-examinations, and above all for the first

one, than that of being in prison. Since I was in some
measure prepared for my arrest, and was therefore not
thrown completely off my balance when it came, it merely
had the effect of a shock which helped me to be mentally
and spiritually alert (temptations to lose one's balance came
later). Physically, regular, comparatively long sleep enabled me to make up for a good deal of sleep that I had
lost; by the time that I had to submit to these interrogations
I was fully rested. The scarcity of food in those first hot
summer days of my imprisonment did me no harm at all.
They simply acted as a good training or ascetic discipline.
Further, I tried to keep my body in good condition by
gymnastic exercises and a morning run round my cell, for
I wanted to avoid appearing before my tribunal as a pale
and unhealthy prisoner. In addition to physical discipline,
I added mental and spiritual exercises. I tried to discipline
my mind very strictly, in order to resist the temptation to
let one's mind wander chaotically hither and thither. I
made a strictly ordered rule-of-life for each day, which
included regular meditation and prolonged periods of
prayer, followed by periods of thought on theological and
ecclesiastical questions. The result of these reflections still
helps me in my work to-day. Since I had no paper to write
down the result of my thinking I not only repeated it over
and over again, in order to impress it upon my memory,
but I also frequently translated my thoughts into English,
or French, or even into Latin, and this, in itself, did my
memory a great deal of good. Under these circumstances,
I could only repeat passages from the Bible, and verses from
the hymn-book, which I had retained in my memory. How
grateful I am to all my teachers who had made me learn
by heart hymns and poems, Greek lyrics, Latin odes, or
Hebrew psalms! They provided me with a treasure which
in those hard days was literally priceless. During those
weeks of strict confinement and solitude I wanted to guard

against a feeling that I had lost all touch with time, so I managed to make a few marks on the wall with a rusty nail where the guard would not notice it; this was really a little calendar, worked out on a system of my own. When I looked at it I could see at once how many days, weeks, and months I had been in prison.

Naturally, as anyone will understand, I preferred to be alone in my cell to being shut up with others, even though it was a st rn discipline, for in this way I received a gift which I could have only gained at the price of becoming a Trappist monk. It is true that a sinister fate was always hanging over me; now and again, though fortunately not very often, I had to pass through periods of terrible temptation, but the fact that in this way—in middle life—I was able to live without any outward impressions to disturb me, through a period of mental and spiritual discipline, and of religious exercises, was a gift of untold value.

Apart from two or three conversations with the prison chaplain these interrogations were the only interruption during these early, difficult weeks. In the sudden change from completely solitary confinement into the most lively conversation of the interrogation (for which I was unprepared) my mind was like a bow which shoots the arrow with double force because it has been freshly strung—so I held out through the first most difficult and most dangerous period of questioning without being altogether conscious of it. Those who questioned me changed from time to time; even when the officials were putting down merely personal details, I discovered to my astonishment how much they already knew about me in the Meinekestrasse. They knew every branch of my activity, preaching, travelling, and lectures. After that, the great man himself came into action again; contact with him can only be compared with the eruption of a volcano! but I held out.

I know that many others have had a far harder time than

I had, and I do not say this with any desire to praise myself. What Constantin von Dietze told me about his encounter with Goerdeler was shattering. He was faced by a man whom the Gestapo had broken, while he was still alive in body. He made statements against his fellow-prisoners, in an almost reproachful voice, and in a very mechanical, colourless manner, as if he were saying something he had simply learned by rote. His eyes, which used to be so bright, had become dull and vacant, showing that in addition to the usual tortures, drugs and other evil things must have done their work upon him. Many of us, including myself, were arrested after a statement by Goerdeler. In consequence, many of us evidently owed him a grudge. I never felt like this, and never thought it right to do so. What did we know of the tortures to which he had been exposed and the devilish methods used to make him speak? It was not for nothing that for months after his condemnation to death they 'used' him. I know too, apart from others, of the diabolic methods of torture to which Gersten-maier was exposed, who met them with an astonishing resistance. I have heard of tortures which, even to-day, seem to me impossible to have been invented by a human mind—no, because in this respect I had an easier time than others—I am not telling this story to praise myself.

I would also like to say quite openly that I am sure that my alertness and inner sense of security during these inter-rogations were gifts, granted me through the intercession of those faithful friends who were continually praying for me before the throne of God. It pleased God, who holds our destiny in His hands, to grant me assistance which was not of this world. In expressing this conviction, I am not being 'poetical', 'mystical', or 'irrational' and 'fanatical'. Perhaps I can illustrate this statement by the following re-flections. Pascal, with his profound genius, once summed up the enigmatic character of human existence in a phrase, namely: 'Man is unhappy because he does not know how to be alone in a room by himself.' Every student of Pascal knows the significance for human life and destiny which he assigns to 'ennui'—that devastating boredom, that deadly emptiness, which rises out of the depths of the Self, and, whether we are conscious of it or not, approaches the very verge of the fear of the Infinite, to which modern Existential philosophers have again called our attention. Man cannot truly be alone, if he cannot be alone with God. In point of fact the tragedy of his earthly existence comes out in the fact that he can no longer endure solitude.

Among us there were some who triumphed over this final solitude with a kind of noble humanism. Albrecht Haushofer's *Moabiter Sonette* are the poignant results of this struggle, which was fought out a few cells away from me. But for myself, and for many others in this building, it was a fundamental truth that we were only able to overcome this final terrible solitude by our meeting with God. At some time in his life, and probably more than once, man must stand completely alone, over against God, as he will have to face Him at his last hour, before he knows that he must be responsible to God for his existence on earth, and before he can understand what it means for our life on earth that the Son of God has hallowed all our solitude by allowing Himself to suffer the final desolation on the Cross.

III

COMPANIONS IN DISTRESS

O NE day, when some of us were busy clearing away a lot of rubbish in the prison yard, one of my fellow-prisoners said to me: 'Look at our group!' and he pointed to our little group of men at work, which certainly included many of the most well-known names in Germany; and my friend added: 'There will be no government or leadership in a new Germany.' He himself was one of the leaders of the Resistance Movement, and was killed during the last days of the War.

At this time, all the chief leaders of the Resistance Movement had been executed. Those who were left belonged almost entirely—either in the narrower or in the wider sense—to the 20th of July Plot. But there were others also, outstanding Trades Union leaders, and politicians of the Left; Count Moltke, the leader of the Kreisauer circle, who had always refused, on Christian grounds, to have a hand in murdering Hitler, as well as some leading Roman Catholics. The two Haushofer brothers were still there; and from a larger circle, several leading scholars and writers belonging to the Confessional Church were there too, particularly the two Freiburg professors, Gerhard Ritter and Constantin von Dietze. Almost every leading politician who had incurred the suspicion of the Nazi Party had spent a shorter or a longer time in this prison. Almost every old Prussian family was represented, and, finally, there were among us quite a number of prisoners whose whole crime consisted in the fact that they were related to one or another of the conspirators. Of course, the degree of political activity among the different individuals varied greatly. There were men among us who knew a great deal more, and had done a great deal more than their captors ever discovered, although they had done their best to extract information from them by brutality and torture; some, too, were wholly innocent men, who were simply victims of the terrible distrust and suspicion so prevalent in the Third Reich.

Among this group were some whose fate is a terrible illustration of the suspicious cruelty of every dictatorship. Most of them had taken part in discussions about the future of Germany, after the long-expected collapse of the Nazi régime had taken place. In the eyes of the rulers of the Third Reich, this was a crime worthy of death, for the dogma of the Third Reich required one to believe in the eternal character of this institution. Anyone who was so unwise as to admit that he had taken part in such discussions fell a victim to the wrath of Freisler, and the hangman's rope. This was the fate of a distinguished architect, with whom Goerdeler had once discussed such questions, but who otherwise knew nothing of Goerdeler's plans. His execution was a cruel judicial murder.

Here, however, I had time enough to think about the power and the historic mission of the Resistance Movement in Germany. I was better known to their leaders than I was aware—thus, as I first learned when I entered prison, Beck, with several of his comrades, had been present at the service I held on New Year's Day, 1944; several of them I knew in a pastoral relation, and the fact that one of the first to be condemned to death asked if I might be allowed to give him the Sacrament before his execution, obviously helped to procure my arrest later on, but I myself was quite determined to have nothing to do with an attack on Hitler's life. It is true that I had long and often reflected upon the Jesuit and Calvinist doctrine of the possibility of killing a tyrant, and I cannot deny that the more his influence pervaded the Third Reich, and the more terribly it drove the German people towards a senseless annihilation, the deeper was the impression these doctrines made upon me; but in spite of all, I remained faithful to the doctrine of the Lutheran Reformation, which excludes this possibility. At this point, there is a good deal of obstinate misunderstanding, so I will merely add that Lutheran Reformation leaders did admit, like the other Reformers, that man has a right to resist authority. It is not true that it is Lutheran doctrine to submit at all costs to any authority, whatever it is, and whatever it may command; such a theory is a grotesque travesty of the truth. It is, however, very wrong to say that the Lutheran statement: 'the Christian's weapon against a godless government is the Word alone', means that a good Lutheran can take no part in ordinary life. People who say such things say them because they have lost faith in the Word, that is, in the Word of God. For a Christian, if he really believes in the living God, what mightier weapon can there be than this 'Word which breaketh the rock in pieces!' John Knox, for instance, was a more terrible scourge to his Royal House than all armed rebels, although he never wielded the sword. This belief in the majesty and the power of the Word of God is certainly the presupposition of the Lutheran doctrine of the Word as the sole weapon against a ruthless authority, rightly understood. For myself, it was extraordinarily important to recognize—as came out repeatedly during my interrogations —that the real cause of the attention paid me by the Gestapo was due to my actual preaching, which they had been watching for a long time.

But in saying this, I do not want to make any judgment upon men whose consciences led them to act otherwise. They have great historic justification for their action. They paid for their convictions with their lives. Stauffenberg, the most active among them, who was a faithful son of the

Roman Catholic Church, was driven by his flaming love of country to the resolve that the political cleansing and saving of Germany ought to come from within the nation, and should not be left to the inevitable collapse and the victory of the Allies.

Of course it is difficult for the man of action, however noble he may be, to preserve a feeling for the background of history; but he ought not to forget that even a scourge may be ordained by God. It is only the tyrant, who lives in the foreground of history, whose view is confined to this present world, who believes that he is his own creator, and that he has chosen his own place in history. And the secularized follower—for every follower of a tyrant has a secularized outlook—also thinks that his master has chosen his place in history. Such men are no more aware than the tyrant himself that it is very difficult to be an instrument of God in history; for usually God destroys them.

Certainly, I was always convinced that Hitler's road would lead to ruin; and that the final disaster would involve both himself and the nation in destruction. Hilty, in his wise, far-seeing way, once said: 'Rogues must destroy themselves!' The plan of God allows the tyrant to follow his way blindly, to the end, until nothing remains, not even the ambiguous halo of a political martyr's crown. Since God has not allowed this tyrant to win even this cheap 'glory', which would have confused the thinking of many German people, He has saved our nation from a certain amount of painful remorse.

Criticism of the leaders of the 20th of July Plot, which began very soon after the final collapse of Germany, was not based upon these Christian misgivings, but upon the rather broad general assertion that here a political caste, which felt its existence threatened, was fighting for its life. I am certain that detailed historical research, should it prove necessary, would show that this idea is entirely unjust and untrue.

But this does not mean that we must not make any criticism of the movement which came to a climax on the 20th of July, 1944. Indeed, such criticism will be absolutely indispensable if we are to understand why this attempt failed, and if we are to estimate aright the historical place and mission of this movement.

As I looked at the men with whom I was imprisoned, it became clear to me that this criticism would have to be very comprehensive and far-reaching. Germany no longer possessed the power to overcome the desperate crisis, represented by the Third Reich, by itself, and from within. I have not the least doubt that these men belonged to the very flower of the nation. Certainly they were not all ' heroes '—some of them suffered too obviously under their imprisonment and dishonour. These were the men who felt dishonour all the more keenly because they were governed by the rigid and external conception of ' honour ' peculiar to the secularized outlook of leading circles in Prussia. The secularized idea of honour knows nothing of that splendid inward independence which faith gives. All through my imprisonment I realized with gratitude that the ministry of a preacher of the Gospel makes a man independent ,both of the praise and blame of the world; hence I have never, at any moment, seriously felt that my honour was impaired by the treatment which was customary in this prison. But for one whose conception of honour was governed only by the standards of this world, this treatment certainly was a gross insult. These men, however, were exceptions, as also were the few who were really afraid. The majority were admirable in their nobility and their inward fearlessness.

Even though the painful verdict of history will doubtless be that the nobility lost the historical leadership of the nation through some incomprehensible failure on their part, and that if, by the loss of the substance of faith they had to pay for it doubly by a deep descent into nihilism, yet during those days in prison many of the nobility expiated their historical guilt with their own blood. In some of them many of the noblest traits of nobility shone out afresh all the more clearly in presence of death, and in the quietness of faith. I remember two young noblemen who were confronted with one another during an interrogation, who, on this occasion, after weeks of imprisonment, met each other again for the first time. They greeted each other simply with a restrained and courteous bow, as if they had no fetters, and they looked through their jailers as if they were glass. This was behaviour in the great style.

Then I remember a Prussian high official who had a very full day of interrogation and torment behind him. In the evening he went into the air-raid shelter, and while the first bombs were falling he said loudly and cheerfully, without bothering about the guards, or the fact that he was forbidden to speak, 'Boys, what a grand time we are having!' This was Stoicism of the best kind. Then there were the Trade Union leaders who had conspired with Goerdeler, and some Roman Catholics, all of them unshakable in their spirit, and victorious over their circumstances. And there was Constantin von Dietze, with whom, in the nights of air raids, in spite of the fact that we might not speak to each other, I was really happy. There was Dr. Walter Bauer, who carried on a splendid and unbroken activity all through his imprisonment; many of us, especially those who had no near relatives, owed much to his assistance. Dr. Menge too, at one time the Chief Burgomaster of Hanover, could not be prevented by any blustering guards from lifting his hat with true Hanoverian courtesy to his fellow-prisoners, and in so doing he helped to turn the prison yard, and our part of the building, into a 'Hall of Knights'.

Still more impressive was the composed, noble, serene gravity with which a member of one of the oldest Prussian families, Ewald von Kleist-Schmentzien, dwelt among us.

He had been sentenced to death, and knew that he must die, but there was no trace of unrest in his spirit; his calmness and serenity were a blend of natural and spiritual nobility. The last thing he read on earth was some meditations on *The Way of the Cross*, which I had written during Lent, and which were being handed round secretly from one prisoner to another.

All these men were most dignified in their attitude, and their courage in face of death commands our wholehearted admiration. But, among them all, there was no one who could oppose Hitler with equal astuteness. Certainly the leading men of the Resistance Movement were all dead already: Beck, who was a great and intelligent man; York von Wartenburg and Fritz von der Schulenburg, two chivalrous figures to the very end; the noble Adam von Trott; and the most energetic of them all, Stauffenberg, who was like a flaming torch. They had fine heads, open faces, spare, almost ascetic features. They had the faces of scholars, these representatives of a high and ancient culture. They could never for one moment be confused with mercenaries and 'climbers', or even with those blind fanatics, who willingly took the places which these men had vacated as a protest, but *the* great, daring opponent of Hitler was not amongst them.

Although their ethical will was pure, and their personal courage was without reproach, the movement as a whole had not sufficient vigour and resolution. The whole nation was too deeply impregnated with the way of thought which had been made possible only by the Third Reich. The will of individuals could not check the avalanche which was gathering pace, and, with the power of an elemental force, had to work itself out and fulfil its destiny. It is characteristic of this uncanny, 'demonic' period of German history, that it came to an end without any great figure emerging as Hitler's opponent.

Months later, by accident, I saw the leaders of the Third Reich in the dock at Nuremberg, and I was horrified, not primarily because so many of them had become old, tired and insignificant men, but because they were neither one thing nor the other: neither the ardent champions of an idea which they considered great, for which they would fight to the last, nor the vigorous and decisive defenders of their own insanity and lawlessness. Amongst them there was neither flaming protest nor vigorous defence, and where was their much boasted 'honour' and 'fidelity'? They had proved that there was no great historical opponent, and therefore no final historical greatness, only the ruins and relics of a spectral faith.

Unfortunately, even among us, there was that unpleasant type of fellow-prisoner (although fortunately, on the whole they were the few exceptions), who turned King's Evidence. It is astonishing, and at the same time puzzling, to see how quickly in such a situation human nature can sink to such depths. When a man of this kind was 'drest in a little brief authority', he at once took the side of the tormentors. He was harsher and unkinder than they. No remembrance of his own situation restrained him, and not even in the tone of his voice could he be friendly and human. It is sad how quickly a human being can lapse into inhumanity. But history cannot be bribed, and one of these men, whom I remember most clearly, was 'liquidated' on the 23rd April in the same way as all the others.

The longer our imprisonment lasted, the more evident it became that there was another power amongst us. It was much stronger than that of the common political resistance: that power was the Christian Faith. It was significant, to see how one after another realized this fact; once it was admitted, our sense of its power increased. This was, however, neither surprising nor new.

In the last years of the Third Reich, there had been a

considerable change of attitude towards the Church. The more the spirit of destruction penetrated the national life the more did many persons learn to see that the sanctuary of mental and spiritual independence was in the Christian Churches. During those years I regularly took part in a Round Table discussion which met under the leadership of the former Crown Prince of Saxony, the Jesuit Father George. In this group there were many well-known names: Romano Guardini and Gertrud Bäumer, the Dante scholar Falkenhausen, and August Winnig, Jochen Klepper and Bogislav von Selchow, Thadden, Pechel, Dovifat, and many others, both Catholic and Protestant. It was clear that the only basis for an independent spiritual existence in those days was the Church, and these men and women sought more than spiritual independence in the earlier liberal sense.

Thus the latent element in our spiritual life came to its full flowering during this time of imprisonment—for most of us, our life in the Gestapo prison was only possible because of our Christian life. The Jesuit Provincial, Father Rösch, who was with us in prison, carried on an extensive regular spiritual ministry to the Catholics, including daily Mass and absolution. It is not for me to say how he managed to carry out this service daily without the knowledge of the prison authorities, but whenever I was able to observe him, I admired his zeal. On the side of the Evangelical Church, in similar hidden ways, many requests for spiritual literature came to my fellow-prisoners and brothers in the ministry, Betke and Harder, and to myself, and in spite of the strict solitude of our confinement, somehow we always found a way to answer such requests.

One of the most remarkable spiritual and Christian phenomena of this period was that of Jehovah's Witnesses. Owing to their absolute love of truth, the Gestapo were glad to use these men in various prisons as informers, for in their love of truth, they always went so far that they disregarded all ties of comradeship, so it was very easy for the Gestapo to supervise the other prisoners with their help; in spite of this, we owe them that respect which we would give to the fanatics at the period of the Reformation. Like them, with exemplary patience, they suffered unto death; no other Christian community had as many martyrs. Their strong belief in the spiritual realities of the other world made it possible for them to go to death without anxiety, in the expectation of a better world that would soon dawn. They died by the score, till at last the Gestapo gave up executing them.

Some of them worked in our prison, and it is plain that they brought an element of humanity into our sombre building; not all of them were friendly to the Lutheran clergy, but most of them were kind and sociable. Even in their fanatical one-sidedness they were more human than many of the S.S. youths who were brutal, and in every respect insignificant. And even though it looks as though now that they have regained their freedom their main characteristic is their iron determination to learn nothing from anyone else, I still cannot help saying that we should give them the praise which is their due. They can claim that they were the only conscientious objectors in the great style who had ever appeared in the Third Reich, and this they did publicly and for conscience' sake.

But even in our own ranks, there were men whose memory must be held in honour, as true Christian witnesses. When I was taken with others to Tegel, in another wing of the same prison Dietrich Bonhoeffer had been confined for a year past. Through my splendid brother in the ministry, Poelchau, the prison chaplain, I was able to exchange greetings with him, but I never saw him again. When the end was nearing, he was taken to Nürnberg a few days before me, thence to Flossenburg, where, on the approach of the American troops, he was murdered. When we reached that place the whole system of communications had broken down, so that no further transport was possible, and also no orders could get through from Berlin or from Hof, the last refuge of the Headquarters of National Security. From the human point of view, it was this fact which saved us from the same fate. But what Bonhoeffer endured as a Christian in his imprisonment, and what he has given us in his writings and poems of this period, has become in the meantime the possession of the Christian Church as a whole.

There was another man whom I saw several times in Tegel, and I sometimes talked to him privately. This was the Jesuit Father, Delp. Neither his clothing, nor his somewhat countrified face, which was also the face of a thinker, suggested that he was a priest. He was a convert, and one of the most intelligent and creative workers on the newspaper known as *Stimmen der Zeit,* that most important and able organ of Jesuit opinion. His contributions were familiar to me because we had discussed many questions and tasks together, and had already worked together from time to time, even as writers, in the attempt to formulate our ideas. Like most of the others, he was undaunted and unbroken. The account of the last moments before his execution is unforgettable. He said to the prison chaplain, who was accompanying him, speaking out of the fullness of his faith in eternal life, ' In a few moments I shall know more than you do! ' According to the classic formula of the Epistle to the Hebrews, 'Faith is the assurance of things hoped for, the proving of things not seen '.

One of the most impressive figures, however, was Count Helmuth von Moltke. When we, who were probably destined for death, had gathered in the corridor of the Gestapo prison in the Lehrter Strasse to be transported to Tegel, a man who was possibly six feet tall, dressed in prison clothes, made a deep impression on me. When my name was called out he nodded to me with a specially friendly expression, and while I was still searching my memory to find out where I had seen his face before, which seemed familiar to me, his name was called, and I knew that he was Count Moltke, who had often been present at services which I had conducted. In the green police lorry we happened to sit next one another, and since he was shivering in his thin prison clothes, I gave him my rug to keep him warm.

After our arrival in Tegel we were put in a room and locked in, to wait for further formalities. One of those little human incidents then followed which is only possible when you are dealing with quite old and experienced officials, who know how far they can go. The head guard who was looking after us left us alone for some time, in order that we might have time to smoke and to talk, both of which were strictly forbidden. For many of us, and for myself also, this was our first possibility of communication with one another, and of getting news, after weeks of solitary confinement. Moltke, Stelzer, and I sat together for some time.

I was greatly impressed by the quiet certainty with which Moltke spoke to Stelzer and some of the others. He said—
' Don't have any illusions! If you have done what you have just told us, you will be hanged.' His calmness was not stoical, because it sprang from an inward detachment which was almost cheerful, and he tried to persuade us to give up all illusions about our fate, and challenged us to prepare for death.

He did this himself in an exemplary manner, without the slightest self-deception about his probable end; he lived in a cheerful clarity of soul, the most shining example of a resolute attitude, due to his faith. As a Christian, he was the most convinced and the most certain of all of us. His faith was completely solid and real. He had no trace of that kind of scepticism which is at times only overcome after struggle and effort, even by the most mature and religious men and women. He had already achieved what is only possible on the borderland of death—the conflict lay behind him. No cloud of temptation dimmed his confidence and his faith. I can bear witness that I only saw him cheerful and calm. When, on the day before his execution, the chief guard went into his cell and said, 'Another examination to-morrow—the last one', he only answered, quite tranquilly, 'Oh, I know, the execution', and went on reading my exposition of the *Book of Revelation* which had been his chief spiritual reading during these last days. The letters he wrote during this period are marvellous in their certainty and clearness. Up to the last he was inwardly completely free, friendly, helpful, thoughtful for others, a truly free human being, with inward nobility, in the midst of a world of meanness and cruelty.

Friedrich Justus Perels, the legal adviser of the Confessional Church, also finished his life on earth in great peace. I had often seen him in the courtyard of the prison and had secretly spoken to him. During the days when he was constantly being interrogated, when he was tormented a great deal, he looked much more deeply affected than in the later days when he quietly prepared himself as a Christian for the end. Even though, among all those who were condemned to death, a faint ray of hope still existed, that external events might be swifter than the justice of the Gestapo, he was prepared and he was at peace. The greetings which he gave me to the brethren of the Student Christian Movement in England, to which he owed a great deal, have already been given. His memory is blessèd.

From the human point of view, it is sad to think that so many of these friends perished in the last days and hours of the Third Reich, when liberation was at the door. This included both those who were condemned to death and others, but even in memory we must not let bitterness have the last word, but only the conviction that God's holy purpose was fulfilled in their lives, and thankfulness for the fact that He granted them strength to face death with faith and confidence. We who were privileged to see and accompany these brethren on the last part of the way that they had to tread on earth, are glad to bear our witness to their victory, in gratitude and reverence.

'In the sight of the unwise they seemed to die, and their departure is taken for misery . . . but they are in peace.'[1]

---

[1] Wisdom 3.2-3.

IV

IN THE NIGHT WATCHES

So far as the Gestapo was concerned the nights were not nights at all, for they were neither dark nor quiet. It was not at all unusual to be fetched out of one's cell for an interrogation towards midnight, and executions usually took place 'in the small hours', between three and four o'clock. For the rest of the time the guards did a great deal to make the nights noisy and unrestful by their shouted conversations, or by the noisy way in which they changed guard. The electric light was on in our cells all night long; probably the reason for this was the fear of attempted suicide, or other undesirable happenings. In any case, so far as we were concerned, there was no lack of electric power during the night. Of course, it was extremely unpleasant to have to sleep in spite of noise and light. I was constantly trying to discover different ways of covering my eyes and stopping up my ears, but as often as I found a new method, the guard would look in and noisily forbid it; then I had to think of something else! The most disagreeable thing of all was this: towards two or three o'clock in the morning one of the young men would open the cell door and shout to me: 'Lie on your back! and keep your hands outside!' But such amenities were part of the everyday life in prison—above all in the earlier period. Now and again, I shouted back. Of course it wasn't any use, but *I* felt better! Later, however, the peace of night time was restored, in a wholly unexpected way; and this brought with it inward stillness and the possibility of thought and reflection—for, after all, it *was* war-time and there were air

73

alarms! In the short nights of August, this did not occur very often, but as the autumn advanced, air raids became more frequent, till at last they were quite regular. Then the nights changed their character. These nights of air raids were filled with their own romance. It is astonishing how deeply embedded in the human heart is the sense of adventure! This was roused by the 'devil's dance' of these air attacks.

Outwardly our situation was very painful, it is true; although I had got used to my fetters, I still found them rather tiresome when I tried to put my wash-basin on my head to protect me from splinters! While the explosions were taking place all around us, I crouched down in the corner, right under the window, in order to be protected from the worst splinters of glass, bombs, and flak. We all did the same; but we only did so during the brief moments when the bombs were raining down, with their diabolical whistling, in our immediate neighbourhood. When this had ceased, and the strong old walls had ceased to shake, then I stood at the window, spellbound by the play of the searchlights, which lit up the sky above the quivering city like some grim farce with its sinister flood-lighting! Sometimes, while I was watching the aerial drama I saw one of our searchlights 'pick up' an enemy aircraft: suddenly the shining silvery form was exposed, so brilliant, and yet so dangerous! When two searchlights managed to 'spot' an enemy plane, then the whole battery of light was turned upon it from every quarter; and they held it ruthlessly in their beams, ceaselessly intercepting all its efforts to escape; up and down, in and out went the plane, trying to break through the charmed circle of dazzling light, while from below shells were bursting all round the plane, like sparks from an engine. Rarely did one of these 'sparks' touch an enemy aircraft, but when it did—down it plunged, like a burning torch, into the abyss below.

At the Lehrter Railway Station, which was close by, there must have been a strong anti-aircraft post. When it went into action the constant droning was often very unpleasant; very often, too, the whole sky was alight with the red flares dropped by the enemy before the bombs were released; when these lights lit up the prison courtyard so that it was as clear as day, in the anxious moments before the deadly rain of bombs began to fall, there was only one thing to do: to commit oneself to God, for one can pray, even with chained hands. In this respect we were certainly better off than our jailers. Externally, of course, they were better off than we! While *we* had to remain in our locked cells on the third floor where, should anything happen to us, we might burn or bleed to death without anyone knowing anything about it until the 'All Clear' signal went—*they* went shouting and clattering down the iron staircase into the air-raid shelter. No National Socialist sense of duty detained them for a moment; but when they had gone, and we were alone up there in the darkness, we felt as if their power had been removed; for a few moments at any rate, we felt the pressure of their authority lifted, and we knew ourselves to be in the hands of the Lord of life and death, whose sovereignty was exercised over them and us alike.

To be brought face to face with death gives a certain inward nobility to a human being. The instinctive pride with which the soldier from the front encountered the man behind the lines springs from the same root. The person who is threatened by death feels prouder than the man who feels secure, for spiritual freedom is enhanced for those who have ceased to cling to life. I used to think: if our end has been determined by the Divine Will, then, in the last resort, it doesn't matter very much how it comes—whether by the hangman's rope or in an air raid; and if we do come through alive, this can only be due to a miracle; every day we experienced this afresh. Such reflections, and also the consciousness that during these nights of danger a volume of increasing intercession was going up for us outside the prison walls, had their effect upon us. So I was able to go through these nightly scenes of hell, which increased more and more towards the end of the time, without any loss of confidence.

Only once did I have a different experience. I think my heart must have been in a bad state. The young prison doctor, who was probably not very expert, and certainly as an S.S. man was not much interested in his patients —his assistant did not even know what asthma was—had given me a drug which was obviously the wrong one for me. That particular night, when the sirens began to wail, and all the noise and din began outside, I literally knew what it was to experience 'fear and trembling'. And in fact, I must be thankful that I was able to endure not merely as a stoic, for if anyone wishes to trust God absolutely he must be reduced to the utmost limit of helplessness. He must go right down into that 'dark valley' of which the 23rd Psalm speaks. But in ordinary daily life how can anyone feel this sense of helpless desolation?

These nights of air raids brought me another gift—as soon as the lights had been extinguished, we had to roll up the black-out blinds, in order that they should not be torn by glass splinters, for no new material could be procured, and since we were regarded as dangerous criminals we had to have the light on in our cells all night. As soon as the sirens began to wail and the light was turned off, every time I used to roll up the dark paper with great satisfaction, for now I was able to see what had been hidden from me during the first weeks of my imprisonment—the starlit heaven. Then, for a time, before the noise of bombs and guns rent the stillness, the world of night lay around us, with its consolations and its peace; although I could only see a small section of the starlit heaven from my barred window, which faced north-north-west, yet I could see the Great Bear and sometimes I caught a glimpse of Orion. To me the silent radiance of these celestial lights, which have seen so much human sorrow, came like a message of peace from God.

> *Messenger of order eternal,*
> *Chariot of gold!*
> *Radiant in glory supernal,*
> *As in days of old;*
> *Thou movest across the heavens*
> *Bringing to us in our dark night*
> *The shining glory of the stars.*
>
> *Thou wanderest on, as in days of old,*
> *Circling ever in the eternal Plan,*
> *Giving to us who see thy track of gold*
> *Courage to obey God rather than man.*
>
> *Silent and still is thy glorious course,*
> *For Thy Power shines forth in the glory*
> *Of the Stars.*
>
> *Silently, Thou dost proclaim God's Praise,*
> *The praises of her Lord, Who, throughout all Time*
> *Maketh a way upon earth for His own.*

Another beautiful human flower bloomed in those nights of horror. Once again there was an air alarm. The prison lay in complete darkness. Outside there was still nothing to be seen, but a strange stillness, when everything seemed to be holding its breath in expectation, brooded over us. The guards had gone clattering down the staircase; we heard them talking loudly as they approached the air-raid shelters; and now, in the upper part of the building where we were, everything was as quiet as death. Suddenly and silently, both the bolts of my cell door were pushed back;

very quietly the door was opened, a very little way. There stood Freiherr von Guttenberg; he signed to me to be silent. When everything was quite quiet round us, we carried on a short conversation, in a low whisper. He said to me: 'Don't you think that those of us who are in this situation understand the story of Gethsemane better than ever before?' He was not the only one in this building who knew and loved Pascal's incomparable meditation upon the story of Gethsemane; so we talked together for a little while about the comfort that this part of the New Testament brought us in our present situation. I shall never forget this scene; it might have come straight out of a Dostoievsky novel: the dark and gloomy building; the din of bursting shells and whistling bombs, outside; and within, this whispered conversation about the Son of God, who on that night on the Mount of Olives lifted the horror from every other human night; henceforth He is for ever with those who suffer and struggle and pray in the darkness. Nor shall I ever forget this man: he was one of those who was never so absorbed in his own fate that he forgot the fate of his people. How many plans were made in this building to help in the future the victims of the '20th of July'; and how we tried to think what could be done for the terrible distress of the German people as a whole, which we expected to be the outcome of the War. At that time he was already quite clear that all the advantage which we could gain from our imprisonment in the form of confidence, both in our own country, and among people outside—should we remain alive—ought to be used to gain this help. He had retained a complete capacity for thinking of others; and the reason for this was the simple fact that he was a Christian. His example showed us that kindness and courage are mysteriously related. Genuine kindness is the privilege of great and fearless souls. Most human beings cannot be kind in this way, because they are afraid. Who but a fearless man could have exercised this quiet kindness which he gave us during these nights of danger? For what he did was extremely dangerous. By some means or another, I don't know what—probably by giving a substantial bribe—he managed to remain unfettered, and he also managed to arrange it that during the air-raid alarms his cell door should be left open. As soon as the alert sounded, and the guards had disappeared, he crept out of his cell and opened the cell door a little way for as many prisoners as he could. Of course this had to be done hastily, and yet without a sound; for most of us it was an inexpressible physical benefit, like the 'cup of cold water' of which the Gospel speaks, for in one of those earlier raids, in our part of the building thirteen men had been killed, and many of us were oppressed by the thought of our dying companions lying there alone in their cells, in their chains. If this man had ever been caught in his act of simple and courageous humanity, the consequences for himself would have been disastrous. But he lived in that spirit of kindness that springs from a holy fearlessness. He is one of those who kept alight in this building the pure, clear flame of human dignity and greatness.

V

CHRISTMAS

CHRISTMAS was near. Christmas Eve in prison is so terrible because a wave of sentimentality passes through the gloomy building. Everyone thinks of his own loved ones, for whom he is longing; everyone suffers because he doesn't know how they will be celebrating the Festival of Divine and Human Love. Recollections of childhood come surging back, almost overwhelming some, especially those who are condemned to death, and who cannot help looking back at their past lives. It is no accident that in prison suicide attempts are particularly numerous on this special day; in our case, however, the most remarkable thing was the sentimental softness which came over our guards. Most of these S.S. men were young fellows, who were usually unnecessarily brutal in their behaviour, but when Christmas Eve came we hardly knew them—the spirit of this evening made such a deep impression upon them.

At this time we had a Commandant who was human. Although he had risen from the lower ranks to be an S.S. officer, he had remained an honest man, who, although he was harsh, was not brutal, and who often granted us certain facilities, until, on account of his humane attitude, he was removed from his post. Essentially he made more impression on us than his successor, who, in many respects, was also a decent man.

On this particular evening in the year, this Commandant had made various kind and humane actions possible; for instance, among us there was one who was condemned to death, and was already chained. The Commandant had his chains removed, and his violin was given back to him. This man was a great artist, and his playing was like magic. Presently the great vaulted Hall resounded with the beautiful strains of his violin. As evening fell, I was walking up and down my cell, looking at a Nativity Scene which one of my children had made for me; illuminated by a candle, and decorated with some fir branches, it made my cell look like Christmas. Meanwhile I was thinking about the Christmas Eve service which I had conducted a year before in our Johanneskirche in Lichterfelde. It had been a memorable Christmas: a Christmas festival almost entirely without children, for most families had sent their children away from the city, since it was increasingly exposed to air raids. So the men who were left were chiefly men detained in Berlin by their war duties; or else they were older people, many of them solitary, who were rather indifferent to the dangers of air raids, and did not need to take care of themselves for the sake of other people. In any case, it was a remarkable congregation which gathered in the damaged, ice-cold church for the service on Christmas Eve. As I recalled the service I remembered that I had preached on the words from the Prophet Isaiah: 'The people that walked in darkness have seen a great light.'[1] At the beginning of my sermon, I had pointed out that when we were children we used to dawdle home after the Christmas service, because we wanted to look into everybody's windows to see them lighting up *their* Christmas trees, until at last we reached our own home, and stood spellbound before our own dazzling Christmas tree. This year, however, all the windows were darkened, and the whole world was 'blacked out'. Then I said: 'This year, we older people, men separated from their families, solitary people, old people, must learn to celebrate Christmas apart from all

[1] Isaiah 9.2.

childish romanticism and all sentimentality, for this year there is no room for this sort of thing'; then, with the help of this prophetic saying, I tried to make clear the real meaning of the Christmas message for ourselves, grown-up people passing through a dark and difficult time.

I had just reached this point in my reflections, and had just begun to feel a painful longing for a congregation, to whom I might preach the Christmas Gospel on this very evening, at this hard and difficult time, when suddenly, outside my door, I heard my number called. Usually when this call resounded through the wing of our prison it didn't mean anything good. Too often it meant interrogations, or ill-treatment, removal from the prison, or still worse, but although I was prepared for anything, I really couldn't imagine that they would do something terrible to me; I rose, and followed the guard who led me downstairs from my cell in the third storey. I was taken directly to the Commandant. In accordance with his usual custom he did not speak, but went on ahead to another cell. Before he entered this cell he turned to the guard, and said: 'Bring number 212 to this cell too!' When the heavy cell door was opened a man rose to meet us; at once I saw in him a striking family likeness, and realized that he was Count X. His brother, one of the first to be condemned after the 20th of July, had asked, just before his execution, that I might be allowed to give him the Sacrament, a request that was naturally refused. He had been one of the most frequent attenders at my services, and on the Sunday before his arrest he had joined in divine worship and had received Holy Communion.

Quite spontaneously, forgetting where I was, I mentioned this recollection to X, but the Commandant interrupted me harshly, saying: 'I have not brought you gentlemen together for personal conversation!' Then he added, turning to the Count, 'You asked that a certain clergyman, your own friend, might be allowed to visit you this evening in a pastoral capacity. Unfortunately I have not been able to accede to this request, but here is Dr. Lilje, who will address some words to you.' Now I saw what was expected of me. The Count replied: 'What I really want, sir, is to make my confession, and then receive Holy Communion.' Immediately I said that I was ready to do what was required; and the Commandant seemed to have no objection. So a small silver cup was brought, a little wine, and some bread—in the meantime number 212 had also been brought into the cell. He was the violinist who was under sentence of death. The guard was sent out of the cell, so we four men were there together.

At the Commandant's suggestion the violinist played a Christmas chorale, exquisitely; then, in this cell, and before this congregation, I read the Gospel for Christmas Day: 'Now it came to pass in those days there went out a decree. . . .'[1] The violinist played another Christmas chorale; in the meantime I had been able to arrange my thoughts a little about the passage in Isaiah which had filled my mind when I was summoned downstairs. I said to my fellow-prisoners: 'This evening we are a congregation, part of the Church of Christ, and this great word of divine promise is as true for us to-day as it was for those of a year ago, among whom, at that time, was your own brother—and for all who this year receive it in faith. Our chief concern, now,' I said, 'is to receive this promise in firm faith, and to believe that God, through Jesus Christ, has allowed the eternal light to "arise and shine" upon this world which is plunged in the darkness of death, and that He will also make this Light to shine for us. At this moment, in our cells, we have practically nothing that makes the Christmas festival so familiar and so lovely, but there is one thing left to us: God's great promise. Let us cling to this promise,

[1] Luke 2.1.

and to Him, in the midst of the darkness. Here and now, in the midst of the uncertainty of our prison life, in the shadow of death, we will praise Him by a firm and unshaken faith in His Word, which is addressed to *us*.' Then, in the midst of the cell, the Count knelt down upon the hard stone floor, and while I prayed aloud the beautiful old prayer of confession from Thomas à Kempis (which he himself had chosen) and then pronounced absolution, the tears were running silently down his cheeks. It was a very quiet celebration of the Sacrament full of deep confidence in God; almost palpably the wings of the Divine Mercy hovered over us, as we knelt at the altar in a prison cell on Christmas Eve. We were prisoners, in the power of the Gestapo—in Berlin. But the peace of God enfolded us: it was *real* and present, 'like a Hand laid gently upon us'.

Since the Commandant had obviously done all this without permission, and on his own personal responsibility, he could not allow any further conversation. The violinist played a closing chorale; I parted from my fellow-prisoner with a warm handshake, saying: 'God bless you, brother X.' When we reached the corridor the Commandant shook my hand twice, with an iron grip; he was deeply moved; turning to me, he said: 'Thank you! You cannot imagine what you have done for me this evening, in my sad and difficult daily work.' I was immediately taken back to my cell, but I praised God, and indeed, I praised Him from my whole heart that in this building, under the shadow of death, and in the face of so much trouble and distress, a Christian congregation had assembled to celebrate Christmas. For it is possible to have every external sign of festivity and comfort and joyful celebrations, and yet not to have a true Christmas congregation, while in the shadow of death and in much trouble of heart a real Christian congregation can gather at Christmas. It is possible for the candles and the lights to blind our eyes, so that we can no longer

see the essential element in Christmas; but the people who
'walk in darkness' can perhaps see it better than all who
see only the lights of earth.

> *Upon us shines the Eternal Light,*
> *Filling the world with radiance bright.*

Shortly after Christmas, Count X was sent to a concentration camp. The violinist was killed by the Gestapo during
the last days before the collapse; I have completely lost
sight of the Commandant who, soon after this, was removed
from his post because he had proved too humane. But the
memory of my Christmas service in 1944, illuminated by
the consoling and eternal Light of God, still remains with
me.

VI

HALLOWED SUFFERING

THOSE wonderful days of an autumn glorious beyond compare, which we enjoyed in the prison yard at Tegel during the few hours when we were allowed to be in the fresh air, were also the days when death was most near. It is true that death approached me twice more very closely—this was towards the end of my time in imprisonment when, on the one hand, hunger was doing its destructive work, and on the other, when the arbitrary 'justice' of the last days of the Third Reich (which destroyed so many honest men) threw its threatening shadow over our path. But the days in Tegel were most visibly marked by the grim shadow of death.

One proof of this was the simple fact of our removal to Tegel; for we were brought there very closely guarded; in fact, we were so heavily guarded that it was almost ridiculous—a special contingent of heavily armed special police guarded the prison gates and our own courtyard. In addition, we were always chained, day and night; and the more we learned to know one another (in so far as we did not already know each other) the more clearly we understood that we were *the* group which had incurred the strongest displeasure of the Ministry of National Security. According to my own estimate, not one-fifth of those who were taken to Tegel escaped alive.

Another sign of the seriousness of the situation was the attitude of the prison officials; quite unconsciously, they treated us with that respect and consideration which all well-disposed persons naturally exercise towards people who are very ill, or are otherwise victims of fate. Certainly, some of us needed such care. There was a very old Canon from Cologne, who was so weak he could only walk a very little way when he went into the courtyard for the daily period of exercise; it was evident that the chains he wore were much too heavy for his fine and delicate hands, the hands of a scholar; it was a moving sight. The officials treated him with great care, although they did not do it too obviously. Then, too, there was one of the two brothers von Lüning. This man had a bad internal disease; at night in the cell next door I often heard him groaning. Frequently one of the officials who was on night duty would go to his cell door to express gruff but real sympathy. Evidently this prisoner suffered greatly. I greatly appreciated the fact that, in spite of this, he constantly gave some of his precious white bread to a younger relative who was suffering badly from hunger.

It was this younger officer who was able to give me news of the deaths of Schulenburg and Adam Trott, as well as of several others. I learnt details about the manner in which the Gestapo intended to execute us. For they gave him a taste of this procedure as a test—he was led down into a room rather like a small hall. From the low ceiling there hung ropes fastened into screws. He was made to stand on a stool, with, of course, his hands chained behind him, and put his head in the noose. Then an S.S. man took the stool away and the victim was intended to be left hanging: a very simple and effective procedure! In this case, since it was only meant to be a testing, the whole thing ended with a gruff order from the S.S. man: 'Get down, you swine!'

The prison chaplain, Dr. Poelchau, brave and thoughtful as always, visited us all with great expedition, before they could forbid him to talk to us. When he asked me about my view of my own case, I answered him—being fully aware of my danger—'If I am treated justly, I cannot be condemned to death'; to which he replied, in his astute, sceptical way: 'Justice is a sociological conception!'

I felt that it was right for me to prepare myself for the ultimate possibility. For this reason, these days in Tegel are indelibly imprinted on my memory. They still shine with a peculiar radiance. For here, more visibly and consciously than ever before in my life, I stood in the presence of God; Tegel was admirably suited for this experience.

In this modern prison my cell was smaller than that in the Lehrterstrasse. It was only five paces wide; but it was quite clean, and in these silent days of autumn, when the sun shone through the bars, it had something of the austere beauty of a monk's cell. The more clearly I saw my destiny approaching, the more deeply did I enter into quietness, both within, and without. The world seemed to fade away, and the voices of daily life were silent. There was no telephone to break the stillness; no interviews, no committees, no discussions, no obligations, to fill my day with activity. Even the bars of my window, and the chains on my wrists seemed no longer to have much meaning. My surroundings were of the simplest—just a few necessary things—a spoon and a plate—a table and a plank bed. No longer was there anything to excite me or to distract me. My mind was rested and free to receive essential impressions. The stream of time flowed on quietly and majestically towards God. In point of fact this is always the case, but here in the stillness I was enabled to see it more clearly. In those days it was granted me to tread the shores of that land which lies on the outermost fringe of time, upon which already something of the radiance of the other world is shining. I did not know that an existence which is still earthly and human could be so open to the world of God. It was a stillness full of blessing, a solitude over which God brooded, an imprisonment blessed by God Himself.

And now began a great testing time. First of all, I had to go down, step by step, into the depths. One picture after another rose up out of the past; long-forgotten scenes came to life again; incidents in my life which I had completely forgotten flashed into my mind. I did not know that in the nearness of death one's own past could come alive so visibly before one's spiritual eyes, and I began to see what it will mean, when, in the Day of Judgment, our life will lie open before the eyes of the Eternal Judge like a book. For the first time in my life I understood the real meaning of those words of the Psalmist: 'Thou . . . hast set our secret sins in the light of thy countenance.'[1] All kinds of strange things came up out of this depth of the past—thoughts which had long been forgotten! We human beings are very good at forgetting where our own weaknesses and mistakes are concerned! But what a chain of dark memories is woven when, for the first time, we look back at our life, not in the conventional light of everyday standards of living, but in face of eternity, and, more paralysing and more pitiful, when we look back and see our sins of omission, when we reflect on our failure to fight our earthly warfare with greater courage and resolution. Sometimes these memories were of quite insignificant incidents. One of them was of a fair-haired youth, who was very much attached to me as his minister, who entered the Marines. After his last leave he was looking forward to travelling part of the way back with me, and he had reserved a seat in his part of the train; owing to the fact that I had a circular ticket, however, I hastily took a seat in the last carriage, which was a second-class one. When, during the journey, I tried to go along to find him, I discovered that this carriage was not connected with the others. I do not know where he and his U-boat may be now. Perhaps I disappointed him of one of his last pleasures on earth.

[1] Psalm 90.8.

Perhaps it doesn't seem a very important matter, but who can estimate degrees of guilt in the light of eternity?

To look back at one's own past gives one a sense of utter helplessness. It is impossible to alter it by a hand's breadth. It is over and done with; yet there it is. But it was this very sense of utter helplessness which enabled me to throw myself on the mercy of God. For I realized that I was just as helpless in the face of all my heavy anxieties. I sat and thought: 'What will happen to my family if I am taken from them?' My children had been evacuated to the country; they were in a little country town, with a very narrow outlook; they were attending a school obviously controlled by National Socialist standards. 'It is evident,' I said to myself, 'that the children of a man who is in prison as a traitor to the Third Reich, and who will perhaps be executed, can't have much of a future! The people of this little town can be as harsh as they are dense.' My very fetters were a symbol! I knew I could not lift a hand to help them! What an intolerable situation for an able-bodied man.

Finally, on the same plane of experience I had to struggle to overcome the fear of death. Here again, it was the same sense of utter helplessness—'for what can *I* do if God has planned and determined the end of my life? What room is there for plans and desires of my own?' What was the use of indulging in bitter reflections on the tasks I had left undone? I said to myself: 'Like this cell, and these fetters, here is something I cannot evade. There is only one way to the mercy of God: and that is, that I must seek it at that point which He Himself will show me, since it is He who has determined the purpose of my life. Only if I willingly surrender to his holy Will can I praise Him.'

So, in addition to my rule of Life which I carried on as usual, I added a quarter of an hour of daily meditation on death, in order to prepare myself, gradually, for the possibility of execution. Every day I used to end this quarter of an hour with the prayer that God would not let my knees tremble if I had to step on that stool of which my neighbour had recently told me. Henceforward, I looked up daily to the Son of God, who, in the Garden of Gethsemane, had surrendered to the difficult and holy Will of God, who through His agony and conflict has robbed death of its fears. From Him I learned to endure trembling and anguish, and to say ' Yes ' to this difficult holy Will of God. This is an agony upon which God's blessing rests; this is a holy fire which burns away one's guilt. This is a holy conflict with death, against whose dark clouds the rainbow of the Divine Mercy shines out as never before.

I was conscious that around me were many others fighting the same fight of faith; that in this building many people were praying, and praying a great deal, and that more than one of us was treading this last stage of his life on earth confidently and calmly because his eyes were fixed on the Divine Mercy. I was also conscious of the power of the intercession of those who were praying for me outside the prison. The celebration of Holy Communion in my cell, when I knelt upon the floor, made my own prayer of confession, and my brother Poelchau gave me absolution and communion, was full of the sense of divine certainty—for me it was the inner turning-point of my imprisonment.

Such experiences open up a new dimension of depth in human existence. No one knows the nature of man completely, who has not seen him when he is completely helpless, for then he shows himself as he really is; whatever remains when he has reached this extreme limit will probably be genuine. In any case, at this extreme limit of human life, it becomes clear why God is with those who are despised, outcast, tortured, imprisoned, disinherited and solitary. It is true that He is also with the proud, the self-complacent, the arrogant and the self-righteous, for without

Him and His merciful judgment they would indeed be lost. Christ was also with the Pharisees, and His words to them still conceal a desire to win them to Himself. But the most genuine picture of Christ is still that of Rembrandt's 'Hundred Guilder Print', which represents Him as a magnet of Light attracting to Himself all who are in the darkness of sorrow and sin.

The superhuman wisdom and the profound knowledge of the human heart possessed by the saints, and by all great Christians, spring from the same source. For they see man as he is, in his helplessness; their eyes pierce the armour of conventionality, and as they look at the wealthy business man, or the statesman, with his lust of power, or at a brilliant leader of the Church, they see the real man, who is tired and often uncertain, who is sometimes depressed, or who suffers from a sense of frustration and guilt in his inner life; so they speak to this man at the lowest point in his existence, and in so doing they touch a hidden and forgotten chord in his heart, to which he instinctively responds. For they have spoken 'to his condition'.

From the same point of view I began to understand why it was that the younger Bodelschwingh[1] was such a great Christian leader. I had always been under the impression that his cleverness, which was so much deeper than mere intelligence, might have made him a sceptic, had he not met the truth of Christ. And I often asked myself whether his position as a Christian was not perilously near to absolute scepticism? For he was free from all illusions about man, and especially about man who 'has religion'. But, curious as it may sound, it was his knowledge of man in his utter helplessness which saved him from scepticism, for

[1] Friedrich v. Bodelschwingh, son of the founder of the village of Bethel, near Bielefeld—a 'colony' for epileptics, which has now become a great centre of Protestant Church life, social service and missionary zeal. F.B. firmly refused to give up the epileptics and other patriots to be 'eliminated' by the Nazis. (O.W.)

in his contact with nerve and mental patients, with epileptics —whose sufferings cannot be allayed by any display of common sense—he saw the profound meaning of human life. Over and over again, he saw that every life in the whole world, literally every life, lives on the fact that there is the Divine Mercy. Man's situation is such that God *can* only have mercy upon him. God cannot praise him; perhaps sometimes He cannot really change him, so long as his earthly existence lasts, upon which heredity and environment are exerting their paralysing influence. He can only have mercy upon him. Man can only really exist at all because God has declared him, a sinner, to be justified, because He promises him, who is under the power of death, eternal life. And because Bodelschwingh saw all this so clearly, his life as a Christian had a quality which many excellent theologians, who are full of knowledge, do not possess: the quality of tenderness. His message was so profound because it was a combination of strength and tenderness.

At this period in my life I began to understand that God can only reveal this to a man who is in the depths of suffering and desolation. Hence one whom God has led into this school of knowledge can only praise Him for this experience, as the most wonderful spiritual gift that he has ever received.

VII

BEFORE THE PEOPLE'S COURT

THE day of my trial drew near. It is a curious historical fact that the order for my arrest, which was only
carried out three months later, was dated the 9th of
November,[1] and now my examination before the Senate of
the People's Court for High Treason was fixed for the
18th of January, the day on which the Second Reich was
founded.

Some days before the trial began, in accordance with
custom, we were again handcuffed. The young S.S. man
who had to do this for me was not acquainted with this
particular type of fetter—a modern form of handcuffs. Since
my experience of chains was rather extensive, I was able
to help him a good deal by showing him how to fasten these
particular fetters. Of course, once more, this made our
nights very unpleasant. Once more I went through the
experience, now only too familiar, of constant air attacks,
while I sat alone in my solitary cell, crouched down in a
corner, trying—with my chained hands—to balance the
wash-basin on my head, as a kind of helmet, while I
wrapped the blanket round me to protect me from the cold,
and finally committed my soul to God.

Another point, however, which was pleasanter, was that
we were not brought before the Court unshaven and un-
kempt, as' if we were dangerous criminals, but we were
allowed to make ourselves decent. This meant that we
could shave, put on a decent suit, and some of us even had

[1] A day observed by the Nazis in memory of Hitler's unsuccess-
ful attempt to seize power in 1923. (O.W.)

our rings and watches restored to us. It is extraordinary what a difference external things of this kind make to the bearing of a human being. I felt it every time that I was able to shave. With two exceptions the fact that the guards yelled at me made no impression upon me at all, but to have to appear before a Court unshaven really bothered me. Human standards of behaviour vary greatly, and this means that there are very differing forms of torment, great and small.

A little incident which happened while we were being taken to the trial still remains in my memory. When the Gestapo officials (who took charge of us before we entered the green police van) put their own fetters on us, one pair of handcuffs was missing. Somehow I had been overlooked (this often happens to me because I look so absolutely insignificant!) and the order was given to start, although I was still unfettered. But one of my fellow-prisoners called out: 'One of us is not yet fettered!' After that a good deal of time was lost until a pair of the right kind of handcuffs was found, and we could begin our journey in peace and amity. I do not record this incident because I bear a grudge against my anonymous fellow-prisoner (with whom, in point of fact, I later on became very friendly), but simply in order to show what an effect prison life has upon a human being, and how it can lower his standards. It can make quite decent people petty and irritable, and this is one of the worst by-products of prison life.

Our journey in the green police van, with its barred windows, had a peculiar, almost unreal quality. Without attracting notice I had managed to get a place opposite the door; thus, even though I couldn't see much, I could 'enjoy the view'. The heavy machine of the Third Reich seemed to be still rolling on, apparently striking terror into all hearts as usual. But as I looked out through the barred window

I caught glimpses of ever larger and more terrible desolation in that heap of ruins which used to be called 'Berlin'. Even the building which housed the People's Court was badly damaged. Windows were nailed up; the inner walls had been damaged, and had only been partially mended—all this robbed the Supreme German Court of a great deal of its dignity. The authorities had taken a good deal of trouble to give an air of solemnity to the room in which the trial was to take place, but it was a pitiful attempt. There was no tribune for the Supreme German Court. There was no special witness-box (nor were there any witnesses). There was no special dock (which indeed was unnecessary because practically all the rest of the room was the dock)—the experts, that is, the representatives of the Nazi authorities, and the other people who had been invited to come as spectators, members of the Wehrmacht, had simply taken their places around us against the walls, while we sat in the midst of the hall, guarded by an absolute army of police officials in their green uniform. In the background, against the wall, stood the officials of the Gestapo, the real, though silent masters, in this Court. But neither the picture of the Head of the State, a somewhat poor reproduction, which hung on the wall and looked down menacingly upon us, nor the scarlet robes of the Judges, and still less the brilliant light from two great lamps which were turned on us as soon as we approached the table, sufficed to give a really impressive air to the proceedings. The hall looked far more like a recreation room in a soldiers' club than a law court. Once more I realized that all this shoddiness was a symbol of a slowly decaying political order.

First of all we had to wait in a room outside the hall. Once more I had an opportunity to marvel at that brutality which springs from thoughtlessness. Here the official guards belonged to the law courts; some of them, obviously, were of the old school. Most of them, with some reserve, I

might call 'decent'. But in spite of the fact that in addition to all these guards each prisoner was guarded by two
special police, our fetters were not removed. This was
only done at the last moment before we went into the hall,
in order that we might appear to be free. Since there were
no chairs or forms, we had to stand in rows, in the old
military fashion; this caused much unnecessary fatigue to
some of my fellow-prisoners who were already feeling nervous, especially some who were old and infirm. On the
other hand, they called the roll three times; the official who
read the list made a great many mistakes, because so many
of the names were strange to him; since the people whose
names he called were continually being confused with one
another it was rather a futile business. It was simply a
demonstration of some of the characteristic features of a
certain type of official: a meaningless formalism, thoughtlessness, and lack of human initiative, and also, fear of
one's immediate superior.

In this case, the 'superior authority' was clearly the
Gestapo. To-day I am as uninterested as I was then in the
question whether the Gestapo had already decided all our
sentences (that their influence practically came to the same
in the end is indubitable). But I was interested to notice
that the officials of the law courts and of the Special Police
continually looked uneasily in the direction of the representatives of this honourable firm! Here again, everything
seemed upside down. We, whose fate was actually already
decided when we entered this building, were essentially more
independent and more free than they were; the slaves were
not in *our* ranks!

Finally the great moment arrived. We were sitting, each
of us carefully guarded, and watched by two Special Police,
who had to hold us by our arms without stirring. The
experts, and the others who had been invited to watch, had
taken their places. The door facing us opened, and every-

one in the hall rose. The members of the Supreme German Court entered the room. All who were not accused raised their right hand in the ' German greeting ', which, of course, we were not allowed to do. It was evident that the dominating figure was that of the much-feared Freisler.

When he had taken his seat, and had opened the proceedings, there was one thing which astonished me, because it was so unexpected. The whole atmosphere which he radiated was so completely out of harmony with the dignity of the Law. He did not speak with the decisive sharpness of the Nazi leaders, but rather in the conventional pastoral tones of a Christian ecclesiastic; but I soon got used to this unexpected impression, and examined this phenomenon a little more carefully. I then had the impression, which I gained of many other leading men in the Third Reich: his face had originally been a good one, almost noble, with clear-cut and intellectual features, but it had decayed (as it were) from within, and all his features bore signs of a terrible inner decline. This was the man and the judge: Freisler.

I knew already that jurists regarded him as very capable, and even people who did not agree with them spoke of his talents as a lawyer with great respect. At first sight his professional ability was obvious. He evidently knew the documents extremely well, and he used very few notes to help his memory. But his knowledge was evidently not genuine, and was not governed by an interest either in the matter in hand, or in humanity. On the next day, when he gave his oral reasons for my sentence, he said all kinds of completely irrelevant things. Also he was not above trying to achieve cheap effects! For instance, one of my fellow-prisoners, an older man, when he was young, had injured his leg in his work as a carpenter, and this injury still hurt him. When he reached this point in his description of this man's career, Freisler, in a dramatic way, told the man to sit down, trying to show how human he was, but it was quite obvious that this demonstration of humane feeling had been planned beforehand. Further, he was extremely tyrannical, and easily excited. The slightest hint of resistance irritated him to despotic outbreaks of wrath; and his behaviour was the very opposite of that clearness and objectivity which should be the hallmark of a good judge. He was at the mercy of his environment, and before he began his proceedings people would ask anxiously how he had slept, and what sort of breakfast he had had, and when he broke out in anger, everybody fell silent. The district attorney, in contrast to this vindictive representative of 'justice', seemed to represent something far more humane.

Theodor Haubach, a noble Socialist, had to bear the effects of this anger in many ways. In confidence in the order of justice, he took the opportunity of the final word, which is granted to an accused person, to speak seriously about the background of his actions. But this roused the anger of Freisler to such an extent that he immediately began his trial over again, and closed it, not with the expected acquittal, but with a sentence of death. Only once did this mentality of his meet an effective resistance. Moltke, in his incomparable way, clearly aware that he was already condemned to death, had the moral courage to attack Freisler and the whole institution which he represented. He, the accused, who was already condemned, attacked the officials who were supposed to guard the security of the Third Reich, who, if the attempt on Hitler's life had succeeded, would to-day be standing by his side, and when (sure of the historic victory of his cause) he finished with the words of Luther's hymn 'The kingdom cannot fail' (and in the mouth of Helmuth von Moltke this was not meant in a nationalistic way) for a moment we breathed the atmosphere of a higher and quite different reality in this sad room.

No, Freisler was neither truly great nor truly important. So I suppose it is naïve to think that justice must be as important to a jurist as piety and faith are to a theologian? But perhaps both get altered as soon as they become 'professional'? It is evident that Pharisees and hypocrites are not found only in the sphere of religion, but also in the sphere of national life and the administration of justice.

It is no exaggeration to say that I felt this whole process to be a parody of justice on a large scale. It was said to be a strictly secret matter under the control of the State. My wife, who with her usual courage and resourcefulness had found out what was happening, had to submit to be told all kinds of lies by the people who knew, in order that she should not give her knowledge away. Representatives of all National Socialist organizations were present, in the seats of the mighty. What were all these pseudo-Germanic youths doing in this hall? Before the proceedings began they took away our personal effects and asked us all kinds of personal questions, as though they belonged to the Ministry of Justice. There sat the Counsel for the Defence —otherwise men of irreproachable reputation, against whom I bear no grudge, although here they were nothing more than unworthy juridical supernumeraries. But I had now decided to withdraw the honorarium due for my defence from my defending counsel, who was a brother-in-law of Himmler; in any case, it would not have been a big one, and I had decided to give it to some decent institution, in order that his conscience might not be burdened with ill-gotten gain! For he really did nothing for me at all, and his favourable prognosis, which he whispered to me a few moments before the sentences were promulgated, proved to be completely wrong. But these Defending Counsel, who if they took their own calling and their existence as human beings seriously, must have been more dishonoured than we were—were otherwise, within the modest framework of the possible, not unfriendly or inhuman. One of them, indeed, fired off a very adroit question, in order to save the life of Palombini, which suddenly seemed to be in great danger; this made Freisler break out into a flaming and dangerous rage.

Beyond doubt, the most sinister phenomena in the whole hall were the spectators, well-fed and complacent, who, while human destinies were at stake, were quite untouched; while the trial was going on they ate and drank and whispered their little jokes to one another. It is not pleasant to reflect that perhaps a few weeks later this malicious indifference had already found its earthly reward! But I could not help wondering:'What do these human beings think about the events now going on in the world?' Only a week before the Russians had broken through in force, on our Eastern Front, so that the whole Eastern Front was broken, and the final stage in the German resistance had been reached. Rumours of these events had even penetrated into our cells. What did Freisler mean when he shouted: 'If Hitler falls, we all fall!' Here, in this hall, in addition to the sentences of death there were sentences involving confiscation of property—property which had long ago fallen into Russian hands. Since there was no way out of this extraordinary situation, the spectral drama was played out to the bitter end: just as a gramophone that has fallen into water will go on playing until the waves silence it, or as a merry-go-round with its organ will go on playing in the midst of a fire until the flames reach it.

At last, the trial was over, but before we could leave the hall, and have our fetters put on us again, and before we were taken back to prison, we had to return all the documents which had been gathered for the trial, as this was a 'strictly secret affair of State'. I had often foreseen this moment; a good deal earlier I had managed to smuggle the warrant for my arrest out of prison; now, in a flash, I hid under my waistcoat the summons to this trial before I gave back the envelope, with the rest of the documents. The guards were so fully occupied with the general bustle of departure that no one in the great hall noticed my action. What I felt was this: to condemn us according to all 'the rules', and then to leave us entirely without documents, for the new Fourth Reich which would emerge, was too much for me! Later on, these two papers were the only documents which I managed to preserve from my imprisonment.

However, there is one thing more to say about this day: It was then that I experienced the most critical and dangerous moment in my whole imprisonment—that is, the moment when my sentence was pronounced. During this whole period of imprisonment, I had felt no temptation like that which assailed me at this moment, when indignation rose within me like a sinister, hot wave of resentment. This may seem strange, for the essential question in all trials conducted by Freisler was the elementary alternative sentence of death, or not. If a man was not condemned to death, his 'acquittal' meant that the degree of punishment could not be determined. As a rule, anyone who was 'acquitted' was sent to a concentration camp—sooner or later. The fact that in the Third Reich we would never again see the light of freedom, was made very clear to us, in a cynical way, more than once.

All this, of course, I knew very well, and for a long time I had inwardly tried to prepare myself for it. Even the sentence which had been pronounced was only what I had expected, in spite of the soothing but completely mistaken remarks of my defending counsel. None of these things would have agitated me; but while the trial was going on the utterly arbitrary character of the proceedings came out more and more clearly, reaching its climax with the final sentence. Although there was not sufficient evidence for a sentence of death—which was obviously what they wanted to give me—yet we were all accused of treason, and of supporting our enemies. In spite of this serious accusation, two of our number were only given one year's imprisonment, plus a few other marks of Freisler's goodwill; this may have been due to the fact that these men were insignificant; nevertheless, all the nine accused were in exactly the same situation in the eyes of the law; yet in spite of this, two high national officials were sentenced to six years of penal servitude, and a twofold loss of status, and the others to four years' imprisonment. Legally, I myself, had I not been regarded as a 'conspirator', or at least as one who was deeply implicated in the knowledge of the plot, should have been condemned to a few months' imprisonment only. My deep indignation was roused by the fact that here were men who, in the name of the German people, and with the authority of the Reich behind them, dared to impose such utterly arbitrary sentences. For we who belong to Lower Saxony are deeply impregnated with the love of freedom and justice; so although I was aware that this sentence would never be carried out, the fact that it had been imposed seemed to me to be a fundamental attack on the ethical centre of my personality. It was the only moment in my whole imprisonment when my blood boiled, and I felt a dark surge of hatred rising up from the very depths of my being.

As we travelled back to the prison, all I could do to control my feelings was to make a definite and repeated act of literal obedience to a sentence from the Bible: 'Vengeance is Mine. I will repay, saith the Lord.' I did this with the simplicity of a child. I certainly had plenty of occasion to repeat it over and over again.

When I got back, I learned that my wife had secured permission to visit me on this particular day. Thus it was evident that in spite of all the official lies, she had discovered the date of the trial. However, I was not allowed to tell her anything about the trial, nor about the sentence. This was the only time—really the only time—when she was not as self-controlled as usual. She had a very bad cold, in fact she was actually ill, and she had only risen from her bed to come to see me in prison, and the journey to the prison was very difficult, long and tiring. She could only talk slowly and with difficulty, and it was evident that she felt the injustice as bitterly as I did. I could only repeat to her that sentence from the Bible which kept me sane.

When I returned to my cell I looked up this passage in my Bible—when I found it, for a moment it seemed as if the hand of God were laid upon my heart, for the full text ran thus:

> *Vengeance is Mine, and recompense,*
> *At the time when their foot shall slide:*
> *For the day of their calamity is at hand,*
> *And the things that are to come upon them*
> *Shall make haste.*[1]

Suddenly I felt myself surrounded by the majestic world of God, close to my heart, and I understood that hatred and revenge must not stain His holy judgments. I bowed myself in humility before a Hand which is greater and holier than all the unrest of our human hearts. Three weeks later, Freisler perished in an air raid. Three months later the Third Reich had vanished. . . . 'The things that are to come upon them shall make haste.'

[1] Deut. 32.35 R.V.

VIII

THE FINAL ACT

IN the bitterly cold January of 1945, which we spent in
completely unheated cells, the news which reached us
from the different fronts became more and more alarm-
ing. Of course they penetrated our prison walls, for what
prison walls could keep back the news of a moment in
history when the Hour of Destiny has come. Most of us
were aware that we were approaching the most dangerous
moment in the whole period of our imprisonment. From
day to day the difference between those who were already
condemned to death, and the rest of us, became less real.
It is true, of course, that for those who were under sentence
of death every day that the Allies came nearer was a day
gained, but, at the same time, for us all, it meant that we
were approaching the border-line of our imprisonment,
which we could only pass over by a special miracle of God.
What would the Gestapo do if the Allied troops were to
stand before the gates of Berlin or at the gates of our
prison? According to some rumours, in some places, as
the Allies approached, the Gestapo were humane, and set
the political prisoners free. Others wondered whether they
would simply leave us in the lurch, and not care what happened to us. But what seemed most probable was that at
the last moment they would 'liquidate' us all by violence.
From their standpoint, wouldn't this be the only rational
thing to do—because we would constitute very awkward
witnesses? Later events proved that we all came to the
brink of this final, and extremely probable, possibility. The
victims of the final burst of machine-gun fire, which

destroyed those who were fetched from their cells at early dawn on the 23rd of April, supposing that they were to be set free, were found after the liberation, hastily covered with sand. Albrecht Haushofer still clutched in his hands the manuscript of his *Moabiter Sonette*.

Every day the jailers became more and more excited and more confused. Our new Commandant, a rather strange creature, tended to run round in circles, brandishing an automatic pistol! The guards were sent off to take their place on some part of the broken front and they were replaced by older men, who were used to working for the Office of Excise and Customs. Every day the N C.O.s of the S.S. who remained felt it their duty to be increasingly harsh and brutal to us. One of them, a rosy-cheeked man from Berlin, asked me scornfully: 'And *you* call yourself a clergyman? How then can God allow the Bolshevists to conquer us?' I answered him very simply: 'For twelve years past you have not bothered yourselves about God at all, and you've tried to do everything by yourselves, and now you expect Him to be kind enough to carry the responsibility!' He looked at me as though he suddenly saw that I was serious, and I added, 'I am afraid that some of you will now have to learn what the Bible means by the words: "God is not mocked".' He went silently out of the cell. Then the invisible Hand of God intervened, and arranged things for us. Our authorities began to send us away in groups. There was still one wholly unnecessary bit of mental cruelty. My wife, who had received written permission to see me once more (which, by the way, the Commandant had delayed to give her for over a week) was suddenly told to come and see me off very early on Palm Sunday. She was just in time to see how some of us were ordered to get into the green police van, to the accompaniment of shouts and insults from a most objectionable Police Inspector. This was the last she saw of me before the collapse of the Third Reich. I had to give her back some of the food which she had brought me, because I knew it would only be taken away from me. As soon as I could, I 'dealt' with this Inspector. We were walking over a piece of ruined ground, and he was escorting me. I said to him: 'Why do you shout at us like this? You are here dealing with people, who, if you speak to them reasonably, will not make any difficulties at all, and aren't you thinking at all of what may happen to you in the immediate future?' He answered me with terrible threats, and a lot of bluster, but I simply remarked: 'There's no need to get so excited! I am already a prisoner; I have already been condemned by the People's Court; but why do you treat people so cruelly when it is so utterly unnecessary?' I added that this ugly scene of our departure might be the very last time that my wife would see me, and I said: 'Do you think that God will simply look on and do nothing—if you are so cruel?' I never saw him again, and I do not know where he is to-day.

After some time at Tegel, and some unpleasant experiences which enlarged my knowledge of the police, the Gestapo, and their primitive measures, new orders came through: we were to go to Nürnberg. I was much depressed by this news, for although there were always some among us who were blind and deaf, and would not believe that we were heading for catastrophe, I was absolutely clear that, should we survive, I could not see how we could ever get back to Berlin from Nürnberg. An unpleasant voice seemed to whisper in my ear: 'You'll never see your house, or your books, or your other possessions again!' But as I had already renounced them inwardly, a long time ago—I soon conquered this temptation. Then came another misgiving: 'What shall I do if all communications break down, and I can't get in touch with my family again?' Had we remained in Berlin, I might possibly have been able to help them through the last difficult days. It was very trying to think that in any case this final dark chapter in our lives would have to be experienced in separation. It was not possible even to get any exact news of one another. On both sides we were going out into the darkness, in order that our faith might be exercised to the last. The last period of this strange, almost unreal experience began with our journey to Nürnberg. Almost from hour to hour it became still stranger.

At the Anhalt station, a train was standing at the platform—one of those trains which we can now hardly imagine: so overcrowded it was with human beings who were fleeing from Berlin, as long as trains were running. One section of the train was reserved for us. In order not to call attention to ourselves as prisoners we were unfettered, and in ordinary clothes. The people who were standing in the crowded corridor, and did not know who we were, were indignant, because we had seats reserved for us, and (this is really grotesque!) we had to bear some of the general unpopularity of the Gestapo, whose sign was on the door of our section. Did we really look like members of this honourable firm? Evidently we did, for when I, who was the first to enter this section, went into a compartment, a high S.S. officer who had taken refuge in this compartment, stood up at once and introduced himself to me. I was fully aware, even at this moment, of the unexpected humour of the situation. I turned to the two police inspectors who were accompanying me and said, with a very grand air: 'Please, gentlemen, will you explain?' An inspector did so, and the S.S. officer looked embarrassed, stammered something, and sat down again.

In Leipzig, an air-raid alarm went exactly at midnight. Everything was completely disorganized; all the railway authorities could do was to let this train (with perhaps a thousand people in it) stand where it was in the almost wholly ruined station. In the darkness few of the passen gers dared leave, since most of them didn't want to abandon either their luggage or their seats in the train which they had procured with so much difficulty; so there they sat, helpless, defenceless, just as during those weeks the whole nation had grown used to accepting its destiny, as something which could not be helped. There was no connection between the official heroics of propaganda, and these bitter realities. People accepted their fate with weeping or with curses, but in any case they were defenceless. Our police-guards had to stay with us, but I made the situation for all of us a little easier by proposing that we might at least get out of the train, in order to avoid a possible panic. So we endured the raid, standing erect, and free; fortunately no harm came to us.

The planes were still busy when day dawned. Somewhere or another we had to wait for seven hours—a delay which people endured with their usual patience. We did not then know that this last prolonged delay was connected with events at the other end, at our destination. The great final attack had been made on Nürnberg, which had laid its incomparable beauty in the dust; the railway line had not yet been cleared, so there we sat and waited, waited as the whole German people waited during those days of stupefaction in world history.

Gradually, our journey had been prolonged for seventy hours. Our official provision for the journey was simply two large slices of bread, with a few thin slices of sausage. We had nothing else. Our Police Inspectors produced splendid provisions: liver-sausage, hard-boiled eggs, and all sorts of other good things! A younger official, who had reached us on his way back from the Front, produced some tins from his 'Wehrmacht' provisions; he opened one of them, and there was a lovely smell of good, solid sausage! He was polite to the other officials, and handed the stuff round, but all of them kept to the principle that ' one mustn't give anything to prisoners and certainly not to prisoners of the Gestapo'—and who can blame them for keeping to their principles? Further, we were already in good training. For a long time past we had learned how to spin out a piece of bread so that it would last as long as possible; so we found it quite possible to hold out for seventy hours on two large sandwiches! Seriously, though, it can be done! Actually, I did not feel hungry; for I realized that we were at a turning-point in world history.

At last—at last—and it was already the middle of the night, we got out at Fürth—the train could go no further. The final attack must have been terrible. We then heard that many people had been killed: here and there fires were still burning. In any case the train could go no further, and we had to wait in a curious hall that was crowded with refugees from the raids, with soldiers, with wounded people and with the first refugees from the east—a foreshadowing of the nomadic existence of so many German people. Collapse and change of scene were evident everywhere. Even the line of division between prisoners of the Gestapo and other members of the nation began to lose its meaning. We felt as though we were only going to the Nürnberg prison as a matter of form. But the last ditch was still there, dark and threatening. We waited till the morning. The officials were in a great hurry to get out of this confusion and back to Berlin. As soon as day dawned, and they thought that we would not try to run away, they handed us over to the officials of the Nürnberg prison. What would happen after that? They knew no more than we did. The curtain had risen on the last scene.

We left the ruined railway station very early in the morning, a strange body of prisoners. There were no means of transport, and we had to go on foot. Although we only had a few possessions, as time went on we found them very heavy, and we often had to stop and rest. As we went along the main road which joins Fürth with Nürnberg, in the dawn of this strange 6th of April, crowds of the *Volkssturm* came towards us. In memory I can still see their faces, in this curious morning light—the startled faces of men who were surprised and bewildered—who no longer knew what fate was doing with them, and could not understand it, and above all, who no longer believed in anything. Everything seemed to become more and more unreal. *We* were the outcasts, and *these* men had all their civil rights, but who was worst off? Prejudices and divisions began to dissolve like the covers of a badly bound book, and, to change the metaphor, we asked ourselves: 'When will the overhanging walls fall? And whom will they destroy, them or us?'

We walked along in the cool morning air, feeling as if everything were rather unreal. At last we turned into a side street which led to the prison. The great gate looked almost idyllic in comparison with the gloomy gates of the Berlin prison. The building was Bavarian; not an ugly Prussian brick building, but it was built of this southern sandstone, which always has a certain warmth about it. Our first impressions were favourable. The prison seemed to be clean and tidy, and the clothes worn by the prisoners were much better than the rags we had had to wear in Tegel. This prison contained the cell in which Julius Streicher had once been confined. When we entered the prison we had no idea that a few months later Goering, and the other leaders of the Third Reich, would enter here for the last period of their earthly journey. For the moment, we ourselves, in our modest way, increased the historic significance of this place! No new orders had been received from Berlin, and possibly we could expect no more to come— hence we were classed as ordinary prisoners.

Our stay in the Nürnberg prison opened my eyes to an unexpected and unpleasant truth. I began to see how cruel even legal justice can be in the carrying out of punitive measures, when it becomes a thoughtless matter of routine. The men who looked after us here were old and experienced guards from the Administration of Justice. All of them were Bavarians, but most of them were as pedantic and as dense as any Prussian. The more impersonal the punishment becomes the more cruel it is and also the more futile. Since under the Gestapo there had been no rules for our imprisonment, the daily experience of arbitrary treatment made no particular impression upon me; it was simply the atmosphere in which we lived; I was not naïve enough to expect anything different there; here, however, I was daily embittered by the fact that while the authorities pretended to administer a strictly impersonal justice, in actual fact we were treated with increasing cruelty. All my ideas about the complete futility of punishment (on which I had often reflected) came back to me with redoubled force, and, as I sat in the solitude of my cell, once more, I saw as in a bad dream, that scene in the Lehrterstrasse which first caused me to reflect upon this subject.

There I stood, although it was forbidden, at the barred window of my cell, and, as a Christian, watched the life of the prison. Down below, in the dim light of early morning, I saw several ' companions in distress ' led out for a walk in the prison yard; this ' walk ' consisted in moving mechanically round and round the courtyard in concentric circles— round and round, in and out, weaving some fantastic web in dreary monotony. And as I watched what was happening below me in the grey and misty atmosphere of a very unpleasant winter morning, two points struck me forcibly: the first was this—this ' world below me ' was an utterly alien world; and secondly, I felt that this was genuine criminal procedure. As a Christian I wondered why it was that under such conditions of life I could still be conscious of the difference between our lot and the lot of these other prisoners, for I realized that I too belonged to the category of those who were suspected and despised. When I had looked long enough at this grim drama below me, at these men wandering round so mechanically, noting the dullness of the expression on their faces, as I listened to the shouts of their warders, whose voices were harsh and grating, I came to the final conclusion that this form of punishment was only another method of prolonging the career of a criminal.

Many considerations led me to this sad conclusion. It is all very well to talk about righteousness, justice, and expiation; but if such ideas are to have any effect, they presuppose a social order which is still sound and is governed by such aims. But does such an order exist—now—in 1945?

Where the legal administration of the State has become a mere convention, or an instrument of power in the hands of a small dominant class, then it has lost its force, even in the external sense. No 'draconic' measures can prevent the doom of the Third Reich. Why not? Even the pagan Voltaire, with his clear, cool intellect, saw this point; he said: 'There is one thing in the world which is mightier than all the hosts of mighty rulers: an idea whose time has come!' Since the Third Reich was never truly Socialist, but was fundamentally *petit bourgeois* in spirit, its leaders never understood this situation. It regarded its draconic measures as effective, because it measured its effects by the terror it inspired in its timid, submissive and pliant citizens. But the individual citizen in the Third Reich had already lost his power to play a part at this critical moment in history, or at least his mission was threatened with extinction, because he had fallen a prey to materialism and selfishness, to such an extent that he was no longer capable of making any sacrifice. Further, in the deeper sense, the punitive measures of the Third Reich were not effective because they could not create anything new. By their very nature dictatorships, as the culmination of the Power State, can never convince or attract; they can only fascinate, or crush. Indeed, the Nazi leaders used to say this, with cynical frankness.

So as I stood there watching at my cell window, I began to perceive the weak spot in this penal system. As I looked down at those men below in the prison yard, and at their warders, I began to see that an improvement, or a complete re-education of such persons would only be possible if they themselves had a tremendous desire for moral improvement. For only so would it be possible to resist this organized training in submissiveness, by which all personal will is crushed; but this again would presuppose a moral force and an independent spirit, which is rarely found. And as I reflected on these matters I saw clearly the painful truth, that in this sphere of punishment there *could* be no true improvement, because there was no renewal of the sense of moral responsibility, because, indeed, the victim's personal will was ignored; the system simply aims at crushing the will altogether—the only ones who 'get on well' are the clever, adroit, apparently docile prisoners. Those who are well-disposed, good-natured, shy, but with a real capacity for improvement are ignored; the only things that count are the arts which make a genuine criminal, including deliberate egoism. The penal system is futile so long as it is not determined by obedience to God's holy justice, and by faith in God's renewing grace. Where justice is in the hands of men alone, and there is no ray of light from the renewing power of forgiveness, then the penal system inevitably becomes futile. Those who administer justice in a nation should reflect upon the fact that a secularized system of justice is a terrible thing. For once its metaphysical bonds are loosed, what can prevent it from being lost in the quicksands of shifting human aims?

These gloomy considerations were reinforced by personal

experience; for until we had been classified and our cells had been assigned to us, the sanitary and hygienic conditions were very bad; we were engaged in a continual though silent, struggle with thoughtless guards; further, we had to endure the unpleasant malicious behaviour of the other prisoners, who did all they could to annoy us, as 'political' prisoners; finally, we were under a penal administration which did not leave the smallest loophole for an expression of personality. We 'got through' as well as we could, with the help of a rather quiet and grim humour, and a sort of passive resistance: doing our everyday duties, even the smallest, with the rigid attention to detail of a well-drilled private soldier in barracks, behaviour which roused all the anti-Prussian instincts of our Bavarian guards to fever heat—cleaning our cells so thoroughly that our part of the building was still swimming in the first floods of cleansing water, when the other prisoners had practically finished theirs—and other antics of that kind! Obviously, in these narrow surroundings we could only assert our moral independence in a very restricted sphere.

My second unpleasant discovery was that of the power of hunger. I had already experienced, it is true—during my time in the Lehrterstrasse—that humiliating feeling of hunger, when I watched the shadow move slowly from the opposite wing of the prison, slowly, so very slowly, over the glowing prison courtyard, till it reached the point which (like a sundial) told us that it was time for our next 'meal'; in the interval there was the heroic, and not always victorious, conflict with the temptation to consume the last morsel of bread before the right time. But here I had a different experience. Here, hunger attacked us with elemental force, like a strong man armed, who throws you to the ground. Until now, I did not know that hunger makes everything go black before your eyes, and that you can only rise from your bed with the greatest difficulty to totter across the room. I learned these lessons quite unexpectedly, and from this point of view, if the American troops had come a little later, for me, it might have been too late. But now we were approaching the end: events moved so fast, it felt like a torrent sweeping along, faster and faster, till it pours over the cliff in the form of a waterfall.

It was hardly worth while to try to settle down in the solitude of my cell, which otherwise I valued so highly. My job was to make candlesticks. With the help of an ingenious process of rationalization (one has time for all kinds of things in a prison cell!) I managed to get through my daily task in a few hours; in the time that was over I had opportunities for thought, and, later on, even for reading. But the closer we were brought to the Front, the less could I think or read. Air raids—especially with low-flying aeroplanes—became more intensive and more frequent. Finally, with the exception of a few hours each morning, we were never 'clear'. Then came the moment when we could catch the sound of the artillery bombardment. The last scene of the last act had begun.

Everything became more and more strange and unreal. When Roosevelt's death was announced a prison official spoke of him as the greatest 'war criminal' of all time; then he tried to describe what we would do if our resistance were successful—and this was only three days before the fall of Nürnberg—while outside the prison walls we could see and hear the gunfire at the last German outposts. Then our carpenter's shop received a direct hit. This was a wooden shed, immediately under the window of my cell; and that very evening the authorities intended to shoot some of the prisoners in the prison courtyard. I did not then know that Dietrich Bonhoeffer had been removed to Flossenbürg a few days before we arrived and then executed; perhaps it was only due to the collapse of the whole system of communications that we escaped the same fate.

During our last night, when I had placed my bed immediately under the barred window for better protection against bomb splinters, there rose from the cellar—where the prison authorities with their faithful henchmen were 'throwing' a farewell party—the smell of roast meat, and the noise of tipsy men, while above them, in their cells, hundreds of men were hoping feverishly for their approaching liberation—suffering from the pangs of hunger and the fear of death. I was able to sleep, and I see that one day I shall have to write a theological article upon sleep as one of the ways of praising God!

Next morning, although I had scarcely noticed a change in the sound of gunfire, suddenly, after a short commotion in the corridor, the door of my cell was thrown open, and one of my fellow-prisoners rushed in, with tears of joy running down his face, crying out 'The Americans have come!' I felt quite calm. His tears were literally tears of joy, and he was honestly indignant when he looked at me and said, 'But you don't seem a bit excited?' It was quite true, my first reaction was not one of joy, at least not in the superficial and rather simple way in which my companions were expressing it, with their shouts and their excitement. I was immediately conscious that for most of us the way back to life would be very long and very difficult; that there would be many tiresome formalities to go through till we could really go out into the world as free men. Then we would have to try to find our families, and after that we would have to face the problem of rebuilding our homes—where?

In addition, it was rather a bitter pill to know that we were to receive the precious gift of freedom—of which we had been robbed by our own compatriots—at the hands of foreigners. Personally, too, beneath all the relief and thankfulness was a strange undertone almost of regret, because now, suddenly and irrevocably, the time of trial was over.

I asked myself: 'Has it done all that it should do in cleansing, purifying, and giving me new strength?'

Finally, so many of us were so lacking in self-control that it was evident that even great historical catastrophes do not, of themselves, contain the power of renewal. There is a whole world of difference between a collapse which is due to Fate, and the purifying fire of a Divine renewal. This explosion of 'natural' emotion makes men behave in a confused, petty, ugly way: for a moment, weak human creatures seemed to dominate the scene. Their feeling seemed to be: 'We are all political prisoners—we have all had some idea of a certain kind of freedom, things *must* change! We have suffered, we have been treated unjustly —now the day of freedom must dawn, and the way back to life is once more open.'

For the political prisoners who belonged to the *petit bourgeois* class this may have been all right. Under the Third Reich they suffered, it is true, many of them because they had listened to the B.B.C. or had been denounced by a spiteful neighbour. Some of them were decent craftsmen, and others small shopkeepers, who, perhaps when they were a little tipsy, had made some depreciatory remarks about the Nazi leaders. But they were not the only ones; there were also the dubious people who had been condemned for embezzlement, or forgery, or for other things, because obviously, the Nazi leader of their district or someone else wanted to 'liquidate' them. Doesn't one have even a sneaking sympathy for a man who declares that he only 'pinched' a big case of champagne because he was already against Adolf Hitler? I found that I had to be careful not to allow myself, unthinkingly, to be included in a group of this kind. Was it, after all, so very 'arrogant' when the genuine 'political' prisoners—the Communists—who, in their own way had fought very courageously, who had supported the Reds illegally and distributed papers, or when the members of the Trade Unions and those who had shared in the plot of the 20th of July, insisted that they did not want to be included with such companions?

The way back to freedom was still shrouded in mist. Poets have described the moment when prisoners see the light of freedom once more. Dostoievsky was shaken for life by the moment when unexpectedly, at the last minute, freedom and life were given back to him. With us, however, everything was still shrouded in a thick, dark cloud of uncertainty. Even as it expired, the influence of the Third Reich hung over us like a cloud. Over Nürnberg, the town of the great gatherings of the Nazi Party, the white flags of surrender were flying, and the heroic cries of 'Never! Never will we surrender!' which the hoarse loud-speakers of official propaganda were blaring forth only the day before yesterday, were now silent; but the bright morning of freedom had not yet come. This moment was like that of someone who has been very ill, and has unexpectedly survived the crisis, when it is still uncertain whether he will have strength to make a real recovery and start a new life. This was one aspect of our life at the moment.

The other aspect was still less impressive. There was a hateful aftermath of shame; day after day the officials of the Third Reich were handed over as prisoners to the American Security Service. After they had finished their last days in the Third Reich the following procedure seems to have taken place with depressing monotony. They made their last speech to the inhabitants of the town at whose gates the Americans were already standing—'Resistance to the last!' Resistance? By whom? By those who remain behind, the aged, women and children?

After this speech, generally two days before the Americans marched in, the command went forth: 'Orders to disband.' This expression, to 'disband', must always remain connected with this historical moment. For the people as a whole, mothers, children, old people, the call was: 'Resist to the last!' For the people as a whole there was death and ruins, but for the leaders the cry was 'Disband!'—not one of them perished with his town! Not one died among the ruins! Then came the business of Mittenwald. Yes, all these men who were handed over had become 'soldiers'. Perhaps while they were trying to 'disband' they may have blown up a bridge, the destruction of which wouldn't have held up any American tanks, but will make life far more difficult, for a long time ahead, for the German people. Then they arrived in Mittenwald and asked to be allowed to join a special regiment. The army had to put up centres for them. There they were put into uniform, given their pay books; then, after five days, they were discharged in the usual way. 'After this,' they thought, 'nothing very bad can happen to us!' They were no longer Nazi group leaders or men in high office. The worst that could happen would be to become prisoners of war.

But even an American soldier understands that a soldier who has only served for five days is not a real soldier, and a German who stands by and watches this sorry drama being played out, begins to feel deeply ashamed, for he understands that a man who for the past five years has been indispensable to the Nazi régime cannot now, during the last five days, take shelter behind the Army! For the German soldier is usually honest, straightforward and courageous. Most of the soldiers held out to the last, but *here* there was neither honesty nor straightforwardness, nor courage. These men were a disgrace to their country. And now that humiliating procedure began which covered our nation with shame. With one single exception, that of an honest, decent, and human official in our prison, who openly confessed his political convictions, all the rest denied their political faith.

All these men who were handed over to the Americans were, according to their own words, a group of ordinary, middle-class people. At the outset they all said that they were true to the Church; then they added that they were 'humane', that they had stood up for the Jews, as well as for the Czechs and Poles. They claimed that they had never hurt a soul! They 'had only carried out orders'; otherwise they were 'innocent, harmless, incredibly innocent people!' The district Nazi leader, to whose sphere our prison belonged, was one of those 'innocent' men; the officials (who were almost all members of the Party) stowed him away with undisguised satisfaction. *They* knew their captain!

A Gestapo official, for instance, was so 'innocent' that when the man who was interrogating him said: 'So you were a member of the Gestapo?' he answered, 'The Gestapo, what's that?' But before his arrest he had drunk a whole bottle of cognac, and he now looked rather pale and overwrought. According to his own statements, he had helped hundreds of clergy to take up secular occupations, who were all happy to do so, because they were glad to leave the service of the Church. When the American officer who was examining him told him exactly what his function had been, the man was so disconcerted that for a moment he could not think of any answer. Evidently he could not make out how these Americans could know so much about his past life! This drama, which was played out day after day, and with man after man, was so terribly undignified that an observer could only come to the conclusion that none of the concentration camps were necessary! Goebbels' propaganda was unnecessary! all the fighting around Stalingrad was unnecessary! and a total war of annihilation was entirely unnecessary! This terrible cowardice—where not the slightest attempt was made to stand by the ideals of yesterday, when everything that used to be considered important now fell into the abyss of nothingness—this incredible cowardice was the worst self-imposed judgment on the vanquished political order that anyone could imagine. We cannot even describe the collapse as a *crash*. This collapse was unique. Never has a chapter of German history closed in such degradation.

If ever a genuine national sentiment is to be revived in this bewildered people, which has suffered from raids and hunger, from sorrow and wounds; which has been deceived and led astray, and still faces a hard future, then this shame must burn and burn, for the German name has been incredibly stained. That is the other side of the picture. And in between lay the turbulent world in which we were living. Very naturally, our nervous, under-nourished fellow-prisoners for a moment lost their heads! The prison officials were stunned by the turn of events, and the Americans found it very difficult to separate the sheep from the goats, among the prisoners, the officials and the new arrivals.

Everybody was terribly nervous. But there was one fixed point in this shadowy uncertainty, in this humiliating saga of the breakdown of human life—and that was, the Word of God. I had at last received my own Bible, my little well-loved pocket Bible, which had gone with me everywhere, from the days of my journey to India, and contains so many notes of significant happenings; and now I wrote a fresh note in the margin of the 50th Chapter of Genesis.

And Joseph returned into Egypt, he, and his brethren, and all that went up with him to bury his father. . . . And when Joseph's brethren saw that their father was dead, they said: It may be that Joseph will hate us, and will fully requite us all the evil which we did unto him. And they sent a message unto Joseph, saying Thy father did command before he died, saying, So shall ye say unto Joseph, Forgive, I pray thee now, the transgression of thy brethren, and their sin, for that they did unto thee evil: and now, we pray thee, forgive the transgression of the servants of the God of thy father. And Joseph wept when they spake unto him. And his brethren also went and fell down before his face; and they said, Behold! we be thy servants. And Joseph said unto them: Fear not! for am I in the place of God? And as for you, ye meant evil against me; but God meant it for good . . . to save much people alive. Now therefore, fear not! I will nourish you, and your little ones. And he comforted them, and spake kindly unto them. (Genesis 50.14-21.)

This was to be the text of my first sermon after the liberation. The prison church was full, of course, for I stood before them in gown and bands for the first time; till then they had only known me in my extremely shabby prison clothes. I can't help the fact that it is a Jewish book which speaks of nobility, and in so doing, erected the first small, but strong dam against the waves of hatred and revenge. It is God's Word, and His Holy Will; and 'I am under God'.

Finally, after a long period of protracted negotiations, which threatened the overstrained nerves of my fellow-prisoners with complete breakdown, even this last chapter in the story of our imprisonment came to an end.

It was Saturday, the 26th May, 1945, when we finally received our papers, telling us that we were really free. It was springtime; its incomparable beauty adorned our suffering land, bleeding from so many wounds. This beauty was a consolation, for it seemed to say, in spite of all the dishonourable and depressing collapse, the eternal kindly order of God still goes on, through frost and snow, through summer and winter, day and night. But we were still living in a world apart, and we scarcely got any news from other parts of the country. There were no communications. This uncertainty was a great strain on most of my comrades and it increased their nervousness to boiling point!

I myself was quite calm. The wall which separates the visible world from the invisible had become very thin. It was one of those rare moments in life when I felt as if I could almost touch the secret of the Divine purpose behind events.

Then, one day, something took place about which I had sometimes dreamed during my imprisonment. A motor car drew up at the prison gate: 'Where on earth in this disorganized world in which no one can move about except the Allied troops, has a motor come from?' It then came out that the Bishop of Hanover had sent it—for some wandering soldier had brought the news that I was alive and in Nürnberg. Since my parents' house had been destroyed—this I did not know—the message that had been sent there did not reach its goal. I did not know where my family was. Letters and messages which I had sent out on chance to Berlin and Bremen had not yet been answered; suddenly, like lightning, the news of my whereabouts reached my family. Three splendid representatives of my home church, who had won through with boldness and resourcefulness, were in the car. They had brought me a letter from the Bishop. Everything was ready for my journey back. All I had to do was to get in and set out! We drove through this beautiful world of spring, through this lovely German countryside, amid indescribable beauty, and every changing scene seemed like an overwhelming gift to one who had been saved from death. The land was bleeding from a thousand wounds, but the blue hills and the green forests were still there, the rivers and the valleys and every moment, home! sweet home! came nearer. And then at last I reached home; life had been given back to me, with its opportunities of fresh service; and in spite of everything I had gone through, the rainbow of freedom was shining over my life. Much that is hard and difficult lies hidden in the future, but this is a new day. For a moment, the hour of history stands open; we have the feeling: 'Anything may happen!'

EPILOGUE

THIS is the record of a simple Christian man, who, although he was only a preacher of the Gospel, fell into the hands of the Gestapo, and whom God preserved, as He once preserved those three men in the fiery furnace. During his time of tribulation he had the same experience they had: 'The angel of the Lord made . . . the midst of the furnace as it had been a moist, whistling wind, so that the fire touched them not. . . .'

So it is a miracle of the mercy of God to have been preserved in body and soul, although on both there remain considerable scars.

But he is grateful to his Divine Lord for the precious school of trial, which he will never forget; for he is well aware that in peaceful times, no one will ever willingly tread the path that leads through such a dark valley. He has been allowed to touch that shore which is neither of earth nor of heaven but is irradiated by the dawning light of eternity more than by the shadow of earthly memories, and he knows that all his life long he will never forget how life on the threshold of eternity is transformed. Should he ever be in danger of forgetting it, the memory of his companions will help him—with whom he shared this experience, the greater number of whom have been called to the other shore by the voice of God, while he himself, at God's command, has returned to life on earth.

He also knows what a precious inward independence comes with the sense of having finished with this life, when rough and tyrannical hands had pushed him to the very brink of death. He will never forget the last words of Moltke before the People's Court, which could never be modified by any lingering earthly hopes, and made him, a fettered prisoner, the one free man among the henchmen of a dying régime.

He knows too that henceforth he will never be afraid of any power on earth, for once in his life he faced life as a whole, and came to terms with it. Once in his life, he really and completely confessed his sins, and in the Lord's Supper received the seal of a mercy which covers all that is unfinished, imperfect, and wrong, with the blessed gift of forgiveness.

He has experienced how sweet, how unutterably sweet is the life of freedom, and how precious is life, when it has been given back as a pure grace, as something unmerited and unexpected, no longer tainted by the curse of self-righteousness and self-assertion.

After that royal stillness, in which his imprisonment could do him no harm, since week after week he was able to pray, to meditate, to think, and to pray once more, when he was able to commit his spirit into his Lord's hands, like clay to be moulded by the divine Potter; after that time of quietness, which made him inwardly more free than he had ever been, he will often look back, and will continually ask himself: 'Cannot this experience of the most beautiful and precious gifts of God, on the very brink of death, be given to him in the midst of life?'

Still more strongly, however, does he feel the obligation which this time in prison has laid upon him. In addition to those supernatural gifts of God, he remembers above all those who gave their lives; it is this which binds him. For the Evil One, who stretched out his hand to take them, and against whom they fought a fight which was apparently in vain, but was not so in reality, is still active. This evil is not only apparent in those superficial phenomena which we can see all around us to-day, but in much greater depths; it is therefore much nearer to us, and ready to leap out upon us. Wherever hatred, revenge or injustice are dominant, evil is actively at work. For nothing good can come out of these things; they must always lead to annihilation. Where bitterness and despair exercise their paralysing power over men's hearts, and take from them courage to make a new beginning in the name of God, there, too, evil is at work.

And he knows that the only life for man, confronted by these sinister possibilities, is a resolute obedience to the holy Will of God, to the divine order, the divine law, which was maintained by those whose religious and political convictions differed so greatly, enabling them to die for their faith. It is his hope that this may prove to be a growing-point from which the chaotic confusion which still oppresses our people may be healed.